The Racial Problem in
Christian Perspective

The Rauschenbusch Lectureship Foundation of
The Colgate Rochester Divinity School,
Rochester, New York

_____

The Rauschenbusch Foundation was established in March 1929 at the Colgate Rochester Divinity School in memory of the late Walter Rauschenbusch, illustrious exponent of social Christianity and, from 1902 to 1918, professor of church history in the Rochester Theological Seminary, to which institution the Colgate Rochester Divinity School is successor.

The movement for the establishment of this foundation was initiated by a gift of ten thousand dollars from Mrs. Edmund Lyon, of Rochester, New York, conditioned upon the raising of twenty-five thousand dollars from other sources. An amount somewhat in excess of that sum was secured through the generous gifts of citizens of Rochester, alumni of the Rochester Theological Seminary, and others.

The general field of the lectureship is that of Christianity in its social expression and application. A series of lectures upon this foundation is to be given annually during the week of the Spring Convocation at the Colgate Rochester Divinity School, these lectures to be published in book form and known as the Rauschenbusch Lectures.

The Racial Problem in Christian Perspective

Kyle Haselden

Harper & Row, Publishers

New York and Evanston

The Library of Congress Catalog entry for this book
appears at the end of the text.

. . . to Elizabeth

Contents

The Racial Problem in
Christian Perspective

Introduction

It is obvious to anyone who knows the voluminous and excellent literature on interracial problems that no new knowledge and few new ideas are likely to be presented on the subject. Nevertheless, there are areas of the problem which are still inadequately explored, and it may be that these are the very areas which are most productive of understanding and solution. Specifically, there is a dearth of materials treating the problems of racial conflict from the strictly and avowedly Christian point of view. To be sure, many of the excellent studies of the ethnic questions have been made by social scientists who are Christians and who bring to the problem many of the sympathies and some of the presuppositions of the Christian ethic. But their purpose, of course, has been not to show the Christian view of race relations but rather to throw the light of their specialized approach upon a problem which is so serious and so complex that it requires the attention of many specialists. They have wisely left to Christian theology the specifically Christian definition of the racial problem and its solution.

The lack of such a definition must be charged, not against those sociologists and psychologists who have so ably fulfilled their own obligation, but against those students of Christian ethics who are able to define the Christian view of the racial problem but who have not done so. The writer of these words is a parish minister who knows that he cannot produce that definitive treatment of the Christian approach to ethnic tensions which is so greatly needed in Christian literature. But he does know the need and may by his description of the problem serve as a warranty for those who are qualified to fill this void in the otherwise exhaustive expositions of Christian theology.

It can be shown that a major part of the default of the Christian church in this whole area of human relationships has been its reluctance to speak directly, courageously, and in its own language. Sometimes indifferent and at other times uncertain and uneasy about their own ethical program, those who speak for Christianity in the field of racial tension have reflected and reiterated the best findings of socio-scientific studies but have brought to the problem few of the distinctive insights of the Christian perspective and little suggestion that the solution requires anything more than an application of the best traditions of American democracy. This is not to suggest, of course, that the Christian view of the racial problem need refute or should discredit the findings of the more scientific approaches. As we shall see, Christian students of race relations owe an immeasurable debt to the social sciences. But it does mean that the Christian view of human relations should be something more than the reciting of scientific and sociological conclusions and that the Christian remedy for the racial problem should be something more than an endorsement of the creed of American democracy. As is properly charged, we are as Christians guilty of keeping the principles of our ethic "in the shadow of inattention" to the most serious and immediate problem confronting that ethic.

A young man from Mississippi said, "The trouble is, the racial problem has been moved from the area of religion into the area of politics." This may reflect the white man's unwillingness to face the racial issues in that area where immediate, practical, and drastic changes can be brought about by compulsion. If this is what he meant, consciously or not, we cannot share his regret. On the other hand, his remark may be a salutary rebuke to those Christians who seek the solution of the racial crisis everywhere except in the powers of an applied Christian ethic. This is a rebuke which falls not only upon the ordinary Christian in his racial behavior but also upon those interpreters of the Christian ethic who consider their task done when they have given the best secular views of these questions.

Martin Luther said that "The countenance of the church is the countenance of a sinner." We can assume that he was referring in this judgment both to the formal institution and its officials and to that broad community of Christians who form the constituency of the church. Whether his charge is always and everywhere true is not pertinent to our interest. What is true is that when the white Christian church looks at itself in the mirror of race, the reflection which comes back to it is clearly and unmistakably the countenance of a sinner. This is not, of course, a new thought; the condemnation of the white church for its involvement in the racial problem has been frequent and sometimes bitter. From the justice of that criticism we cannot here dissent; indeed, as we examine the story of the white church and the Negro we see that there is little danger of our being too severe in the judgment we bring against the church.

This condemnation of the white Christian church, however, has usually turned on the failures of the church: its withdrawal from the problem in silence, indifference, and neglect, as though the church were merely the victim of sociological pressures and historical developments to which in a default of its own principles it adapted its teachings and its program. It is proposed in Part One that the major sin of the white Christian church has been not merely its passive default in the field of interracial relations but, even more, its direct, positive, and sometimes malicious contribution to the race-caste system in America. It is suggested in this part that the struggle of the American Negro toward freedom and fullness would have been hard enough with the help of the church but that, in tragic fact, the struggle had to be waged by the Negro often without the concern of the white church and sometimes against its cold and resolute opposition. We shall therefore consider in the first three chapters how the church has been and is the mother of racial patterns, the purveyor of arrant sedatives, and the teacher of immoral moralities.

Having acknowledged their deep and direct involvement in the racial problems of our day and having repented of their own considerable contributions to those problems, Christian people may then appropriately grasp and express the racial conflict and its solution as they appear in Christian perspective. We turn, then, in Part Two, to a definition of the racial problem, seeking through definition such a diagnosis of the problem as will indicate a program of Christian thought and action.

Any approach to the racial problem which employs Christian terminology and which applies Christian principles must be to some extent a lesson in semantics. It does not require long reading in the vast field of racial studies nor deep contemplation of the subject to discover the fact that much of our ignorance, confusion, and disagreement stems from an inadequate definition of terms. This is immediately evident in any popular debate of the racial issues. Therefore our understanding of the nature of the problem and the possibilities for its solution is greatly hampered by the fact that words, the instruments of thought and communication, lose in general usage their sharp and helpful meanings. And the handiest words, such as *race, prejudice, discrimination, segregation, integration,* are the very ones which are no longer coins for an exact exchange of ideas but merely slugs which jam the machines of thought and communication. Consequently the language in which racial issues are discussed needs clarification.

In Chapter 4 we shall consider some of the many definitions of prejudice, show their inadequacy from the point of view of Christian theology, and add some Christian reflections on the nature of prejudice. Then, in the three chapters which follow, we shall seek the meaning of discrimination, segregation, and stereotyping in the Christian view. Needless to say, we shall be concerned with something more than the academic or theoretical definition of words. But our purpose in these chapters is primarily to define the racial problem, opening upon it windows which admit the particular insights of Christian opinion.

Not only must we set the four areas of our concern—prejudice, discrimination, segregation, and stereotyping—in separate categories but we must also see that prejudice is sharply distinguished from the other three. We are dealing with the generally recognized fact that racial prejudice is a problem of immense proportions and intense human involvements with which the Christian church is or ought to be greatly concerned. By the very nature of the problem that concern must be dual. The fact that the issue is one of prejudice indicates that it has the quality of inwardness, that in depth it is personal; the fact that it is racial implies that it has the quality of outwardness, that in scope it is social. Inasmuch as the purview of the Christian ethic is "all men and the whole man," the Christian must approach the knotty questions of racial prejudice from two directions—from without and from within. He must understand the *modus operandi* of prejudice, its social expressions in discrimination, segregation, and stereotyping, its effects upon its victims, and the possibilities for the removal of those cultural blights which are its products. But he must also know the nature of prejudice itself, its effect upon its subject, and those alterants which, working within the individual man, remove prejudice as a dominant and primary motivation.

It is well to keep this distinction clearly in mind as we ask of racial prejudice what it is, what it does, and how it may be undone. The descriptions which apply to the genesis of prejudice as an internal and emotional problem do not, however accurate, define the effects of prejudice in the social order; on the other hand, social facts are strictly limited to an interpretation of social facts and cannot explain the conduct of men. Moreover, the spirit of man yields only to persuasion; it is not coerced, either by educa-

15

tion, by law, by violence, or by the shuffling of social patterns, into being what it does not want to be. To say, as it is so often said, that education alone can end prejudice, or that the remedy for prejudice is the alteration of the structures of society, is to reveal a naïve optimism about the human soul and a gross ignorance of the depth and tenacity of evil in the soul of man. Yet, on the other hand, to echo the Sumnerian error that stateways cannot change folkways, to plead in resignation that civil justice must wait upon the universal grass-roots conversion of all men to the ways of Christian love, to parrot the cliché which hopefully declares that morals cannot be legislated is to betray an unwarranted despair about the human situation, a pessimism that ignores the progress already made in the field of human relations despite the prejudice lodged so securely in the hearts of all man. Our division of this part, therefore, makes us concerned first about the prejudiced: the nature of their affliction, what prejudice does in their lives, and how they may be liberated from the bonds of their affliction. And we are concerned secondly and more extensively about the victims of prejudice: what it does to and in their lives and how they may be rescued and protected from the visible and invisible wounds which they receive from racial oppression. We shall therefore make in these middle chapters such definitions of the racial problem as will indicate its depth and scope.

In Part Three we shall apply the insights of the Christian ethic to the problem as it has been defined, considering the bonds of interracial unity. It would be erroneous and misleading to suggest that there is a specific Christian ethic for race relations or that there is a need for such an ethic. Obviously, what is needed is simply that the whole imperative of Christian morality be applied to all men irrespective of those distinctions which place men in superficial classifications of race, color, and social status. The whole problem of ethical relationships between members of the two races could be summarized in the platitudinous statement that what is required of man is required of the Negro and that what is due to man is due to the Negro. But the great fault in white Christian morality follows a racial line; that is, the unrighteousness which the white Christian practices toward some white people, in random and sporadic instances, he is apt to direct consistently and universally against all Negroes regardless of what any one of them may be individually. It follows, therefore, that what the white Christian needs is not merely another review of the items of the Christian ethic but rather such insights and convictions as will urge him to include the Negro in the purview of that ethic. No repeated drilling of Christian concepts of morality into the minds and hearts of white people will avail if to each item of the ethical code the white man automatically adds the invisible and perhaps unconscious suffix, "the Negro excepted." We see, then, that the error of the white man in his relationship to the Negro cannot be thoroughly corrected until he accepts the Negro as man.

Furthermore, we need to ask whether the Christian ethic has any special, even unique, word to say on the subject of human unity. Do we merely put the Christian label on secular prescriptions for interracial harmony or is there a specific peace which the world cannot give? It is here, probably more than anywhere else, that the distinctive witness of the Christian faith has been obscured, not only by secularists, but also by those who have sought Christian answers to the problems of racial division. We must therefore ask what is the Christian view of the bond of interracial unity.

Finally, we shall examine some of the difficulties involved in removing from the sinful countenance of the church those open, ugly wounds left upon it by racial division. Are there forces other than racial prejudice and racial custom prolonging the racially divided church? What are these nonracial yet divisive forces and how are we to cope with them? What is indicated by the relatively rapid desegregation of Roman Catholic churches when that record is contrasted with a relatively slow progress toward desegregation in Protestant churches? What changes, if any, must occur in the Protestant concept of the nature of the church as well as in the spirit of its people if union of the races within the church is to be achieved? However much Christians on both sides of the racial line may deplore the cleavage which now exists between Negro and white Christians and between their churches, it will be evident that there is no quick and easy way to erase the lines of separation. A full knowledge of all the forces perpetuating the racial division in American Christianity will not only help to explain the delay in our progress toward a racially united church but also help to reduce that delay. It will therefore be our purpose in this final chapter to examine such forces.

I wish to add a personal note to this introduction, a note to relatives and friends. As a white Southerner who has behind him eight known generations of South Carolina ancestors and whose children, though born in Northern states, qualify for membership in most patriotic Southern societies, I find myself resenting some of the statements which I have made; but as a Christian I cannot view those same statements either as unjust or as unfair. Many of the references and illustrations which are used here are regional in character, but I have taken pains to stress the fact that racial prejudice and its attendant vices are not sectional but nation-wide. I have drawn many illustrations from the South simply because it is there that the problem is most acute and most extensively and dramatically presented and because this is the section of the country which I know best. I have no particular desire to defend or to exonerate those who are most deeply enmeshed in the problem nor, on the other hand, do I want to castigate them for sins of spirit and deed which are common to all men. I have used the abundant material which is at hand. If it seem disproportionately regional, the hope is that this will not blind the Southern reader to the themes and issues which are illustrated and will not encourage any white American to dismiss the racial problem as a localized issue for which he is not guilty and for which he has no responsibility.

Someone will ask, "What about the guilt and responsibility of the Negro?" As a white man I have not considered it my duty or my privilege to criticize the Negro or to exhort him. I am not unaware of the fact that the Negro as a man is a sinful creature, whatever else we may say about him, and that he is subject to those same passions of prejudice which are native to all men; nor am I ignorant of the "marks of oppression," citing as I must some of the disfigurements which oppression has left upon the personality of the Negro. Where there is a sincere desire to know all of the sociological and psychological facts and their implications and where such facts are uncovered objectively and without malice, questions about the Negro's role can be properly raised; but, in my opinion, it will for a long time be grossly unbecoming of the white man to cite as though in rebuttal the failures of the Negro or his peculiar contributions to racial tension. The duty of the white man is to undo as rapidly and as completely as possible the wrong he has done the Negro. Such a program would keep him fully occupied for many years and he could then safely leave to the able and conscientious prophets of the Negro race, of whom there are many, whatever chastisement and correction the Negro may need. This, of course, will not satisfy those white people who want to shift the blame from themselves to the Negro or who would enjoy public humiliations of the Negro; but the white man can in no other way give the Negro an evidence of good faith.

It will be quickly evident to the reader that this is "protest writing"; quite plainly it is not a sociological or historical survey of the racial problem but an attempt to declare from a Christian point of view what the situation is and what Christian people ought to do about it. I have sought to be accurate, but I have had no desire to be objectively and dispassionately detached from the subject. "Protest writing," writing which has to any extent a prophetic tone, is liable to two temptations. For one, it is tempted to be overly censorious. I have tried, therefore, in the writing of these words to keep a maxim, which I believe comes from Dean Inge, whispering in my ear: "Personalize your sympathies; depersonalize your antipathies." Secondly, "protest writing" is tempted to be self-righteous. I have, therefore, frequently reminded myself that no white man can speak or write about the problems of the Negro with a perfectly clear conscience; and, in my other ear, I have often heard the words of Wilberforce: "I mean not to accuse anyone, but to take the shame upon myself in common with the whole of my people."

Wherever possible quotations are acknowledged and are used with permission. Unless otherwise noted, quotations from the Bible are from the Revised Standard Version and are used by permission of the copyright owners, the National Council of the Churches of Christ in the U.S.A. I have, of course, received assistance from many sources; but I am especially indebted to the following: to Dr. Wilbour E. Saunders, President of Colgate Rochester Divinity School, and Dr. Winthrop S. Hudson, Chairman of the Ayer-Rauschenbusch Committee, for the invitation to give these lectures; to the Kanawha County Public Library of Charleston, West Virginia, and to my brother, Clyde Haselden, librarian of Baldwin-Wallace College of Berea, Ohio, for their help in developing a reading list; to The Christian Century Foundation for permission to quote from an article of mine published originally in *The Christian Century;* to the ministerial staff of The Baptist Temple for the exceptional burdens which they carried during the time this work was being prepared; to the members of The Baptist Temple for the courtesies extended to me by the church; and, most of all, to my wife for her patient and repeated reading of the manuscript and for her advice and encouragement.

KYLE HASELDEN

Charleston, West Virginia
January 1, 1959

Part One
The Countenance of the
Church in the
Mirror of Race

1.

Mother of Racial Patterns

In those days they shall no longer say:
   "The fathers have eaten sour grapes,
      and the children's teeth are set on edge."
But every one shall die for his own sin;
each man who eats sour grapes,
his teeth shall be set on edge.

—JEREMIAH 31:29–30

As we look at the Christian church in the mirror of race, we are struck first by the obvious fact that it is a divided church, split cleanly and almost completely along racial lines. We must discover, therefore, whether the racially divided church is merely a victim of sociological pressures or whether the church has had a large hand in forming those patterns of segregation which are prevalent in society as well as those of which it is itself guilty. Two limitations keep this inquiry within fitting bounds: first, we are presently concerned with the fact that most white Christian churches are racially exclusive and not with the concomitant fact that there are separate Negro and white denominations. The existence of two churches distinguished by a racial line, even though traffic across that line is as open to Negroes as it is to whites, has serious effects which we must consider later; but the fact that the line is drawn by the white man against the Negro constitutes the sin of segregation within the Christian church. Second, we limit this present inquiry by making it a diagnosis rather than a prescription. Near the close of this work we shall turn to a study of what is involved in the integration of Negroes and whites within the same Christian church.

It must be seen at the beginning that segregation within the church has had a long history. A recent study by a recognized authority in the field of race relations gives an excellent and accurate record of incidences of ante-bellum integration of Negroes and whites in the churches. The author declares that he is "stating the plain facts rather than trying to make a case for ante-bellum Christians."[1] Yet the plain and true facts which he states are a mere fragment of the total canvas of race relations in pre-Civil War days. We must have the whole picture, and we must not accept what selected statistics imply without a searching out of the human motivations lying behind those statistics. This author's commendable purpose was to argue from the facts selected that what once was could now be and that the integration of the races in worship would be merely a return to what was best in the ante-bellum customs of the church. But those who are confronted by such arguments for the integration of Negroes and whites in Christian churches will be correct in replying, "That was different!" It *was* different; the integration of Negroes and whites in common worship in the days before the Civil War was, as we shall see, nothing more than a facet of a master-slave society. And it was so different from what it should have been that it made the separation of Negro Christians and white Christians inevitable.

Let us start with the fact that there was integration of Negroes and whites in Christian churches from the beginning of slavery until a year following the Civil War. This was true all along the

[1] W. D. Weatherford, *American Churches and the Negro*, The Christopher Publishing House, Boston, 1957, p. 17.

coastline; but the more dramatic and surprising examples come
to us from the South Atlantic States. The First Baptist Church in
Norfolk, Virginia, was a mixture of black and white in 1800.
White members withdrew in 1817 to form the Cumberland
Street Baptist Church, a mixed church thus being parent to a white
church.[2] "In Richmond . . . numbers of free Negroes attended
the white First Baptist Church, erected in 1802, which housed a
congregation organized in 1780 and which became exclusively
Negro (now First African Baptist Church) in 1841, when another
building was erected for whites alone."[3] In Georgia after slaves
were legally admitted in 1750, Negro slaves were allowed or compelled to attend Christian services under the direction of a Protestant minister. (The word *compelled* is significant.) "On the roll of
members of the Sardis Baptist Church, Wilkes County, (Georgia)
there was a 'list of the Black Brethren in fellowship' from 1805–
1824. Among the forty-six members so listed were such names as
'Harper's Hannah, Gibson's Sal, Callaway's Sip (Scipio), Ronton's
Becky.' "[4] (The possessive case is significant.) It is also true that
there were white and mixed congregations served by Negro ministers in the days of slavery. In Virginia, for example, the Glouces-
ter Baptist Church (white), losing its white pastor by death,
called Rev. William Lemon in 1776, "not white in complexion
though he had been washed in the laver of regeneration."[5] And it
was not a rare thing for Negro preachers to preach before white
congregations. Such illustrations, drawn from several sources,
could be multiplied to some length. Nevertheless, they give a partial and erroneous picture.

First of all, however many and casual were the physical and
social relationships which prevailed between Negroes and whites
in the South in ante-bellum days—undoubtedly considerable—

[2] *The Negro in Virginia,* Writers' Program of Work Projects Administra-
tion, Hastings House, New York, 1940, pp. 103–104.

[3] *Ibid.,* p. 104.

[4] Ralph Betts Flanders, *Plantation Slavery in Georgia,* The University of
North Carolina Press, Chapel Hill, 1933, p. 174.

[5] *The Negro in Virginia,* p. 104.

they prevailed in a master-slave setting. The associations were paternalistic and largely contemptuous of the personality of the Negro; the Negro remained subordinate, subservient, and dependent. When we have glossed the story all that we can, it is still a master-slave relationship. The human intimacies between owner and owned under the slave system were relationships in which the personality of the white man was inflated by the power to possess and dominate another life and in which the personality of the Negro was smothered by his being possessed and dominated. Erich Fromm has said, in *The Art of Loving*, that "Love is union under the condition of preserving one's integrity."[6] In the most extremely indulgent and touching master-slave relationships on record, those rare stories of which sentimental novels are made, the relationship of Negro and white was not union, and the integrity of the Negro was not preserved.

Secondly, in this regard we must note that the inclusion of Negroes, both free and slave, in white churches was plainly prudential. As early as 1715 it was thought, and correctly, that an exclusively Negro church might become a center for conspiracy. *The Laws Concerning Servants and Slaves*, a revision for the colony of North Carolina in 1715, read: "Be it further enacted, That if any master, or owner of negroes, or slaves, or any other person or persons whatsoever in the government shall permit or suffer any negro or negroes to build on their or either of their lands or any part thereof any house under pretense of a meeting house upon account of worship or upon any pretense whatsoever, and shall not suppress and hinder them, he, she, or they so offending shall for every default forfeit and pay fifty pounds, one-half towards defraying the contingent charges of the government, the other to him or them that shall sue for the same."[7] Such stringent codes were later ignored or relaxed and Negroes were permitted the right to as-

[6] Erich Fromm, *The Art of Loving*, Harper & Brothers, New York, 1956, p. 20.

[7] John S. Bassett, *Slavery and Servitude in North Carolina*, Johns Hopkins University Studies, Vol. XIV, Baltimore, 1896, p. 50. (Quoted from *Laws of 1715*, Ch. 46, Sect. 18.)

semble in worship, but usually under the watchful eye of at least one white attendant. But after the Vesey Plot in Charleston, South Carolina, in 1822, and the Nat Turner Rebellion in Southampton County, Virginia, in 1831, the assembling of purely Negro congregations and the use of Negro preachers were forbidden. "The Christianizing influence had seemingly been too effective. Negro preachers had 'distorted' the Bible into a guide to freedom, and the safety of the institution was seen to hinge on the purging of such 'heresy' from the minds of slaves. The legislature [Virginia] decreed that 'no slave, free negro, or mulatto shall preach, or hold any meeting for religious purposes either day or night.' "[8]

So what appears on the surface to be "the very best tradition of the old South" proves upon examination to be a diplomacy by which the Christian could ease his conscience by giving the Negro the Gospel while at the same time preventing an insurrection against slavery. But it could hardly be expected that a church, preaching a gospel which declared the Negro essentially inferior to the white man and slavery a divine decree and using a Biblical basis for such arguments, would at the same time welcome and entertain the Negro even on the basis of spiritual equality.

What is of more interest to us is not the fact that there was a kind of integration in the ante-bellum church but the fact that segregation of the races had its beginning in the church quite as early as its emergence in secular society. The exact site of the ecclesiastical birth of segregation is disputed; but, however clouded its beginnings, it is a fact that Jim Crowism had some of its first expressions in the church. One of the earliest dates gives the distinction to Savannah, Georgia. An all-Negro church was formed in Savannah by George Liele in 1779. This church later became a mixed church, then reverted to being a Negro church, and thus became the beginning of Negro Baptist work in Georgia.[9] Undoubtedly there were numerous instances of friction between

[8] *The Negro in Virginia*, p. 105.
[9] John Hope Franklin, *From Slavery to Freedom*, Alfred A. Knopf, New York, 1948, p. 161.

27

Negro and white Christians from the beginning, and it is evident that the white Christians, who had command of the situation, early imposed restrictions on the Negro members of the mixed churches. An important point is that while the South, for whatever reason, continued to include its slaves in common worship, the North began to segregate free Negroes from whites in public worship during Colonial days. Where a master-slave relationship did not exist to maintain status between Negroes and whites within the same church, artificial distinctions arose; and they arose first, not between masters and slaves, but between whites and freedmen.

C. Vann Woodward, in a book called *The Strange Career of Jim Crow,* has firmly established the fact that segregation, as we know it today, is of rather recent origin. He cites a series of interesting and significant facts: "More than a decade was to pass after Redemption (the end of the era of reconstruction) before the first Jim Crow law was to appear upon the law books of a Southern state."[10] In 1879 Sir George Campbell, a member of Parliament, traveling in the South, commented "with particular surprise on the equality with which Negroes shared public facilities."[11] In 1898 the Charleston, South Carolina, *News and Courier* ridiculed the suggestion that the Negro be segregated, pointing out the impracticalities involved; but within ten years after the dawn of the present century nearly all of the Southern states had perfected in custom and law an almost complete ostracism of the Negro. The earliest date established by Woodward for the beginning of racial segregation in the South was 1877, with the withdrawal of the Federal troops and "the acquiescence of the rest of the country in the South's demand that the whole problem be left to the disposition of the dominent Southern white people."[12] His thesis, well argued, is that systematized social segregation as we know it today is a relatively new thing in American culture.

[10] C. Vann Woodward, *The Strange Career of Jim Crow,* Oxford University Press, New York, 1955, p. 16.
[11] *Ibid.,* p. 18.
[12] *Ibid.,* p. 6.

What needs to be emphasized, however, is that the segregation of the races had occurred in the Christian churches at least as early as it had appeared in its secular forms. Woodward is aware of the fact that the racial division of the Protestant churches had already come about before the end of Reconstruction, suggesting that this happened during "the First Reconstruction . . . by the voluntary withdrawal of the Negroes."[13] But he is referring here not to segregation within the churches but to the separation of the churches. What we must see is that discrimination against the Negro, free and slave, had begun in the North and in the South nearly a century earlier and that the "voluntary" withdrawal of the Negro had been forced by the embarrassments to which he had been put in mixed churches, an evidence that the church did not merely inherit or absorb the patterns of an evil society but in fact helped provide those patterns. The chronological sequence is vital to a correct understanding of what actually happened. First came the segregation of the Negro within the church; then followed the separation of the churches by the "spontaneous" withdrawal of the Negro Christians; much later, the elaborate patterns of segregation were to arise in the church and in secular society.

Long before the little signs—"White Only" and "Colored"— appeared in the public utilities they had appeared in the church. This is not a mere figure of speech. In 1795 the John Street Methodist Episcopal Church in New York City, a mixed church including whites and both free and slave Negroes, was divided when the Negroes under the leadership of a former slave, Peter Williams, who had purchased his freedom through the church's aid, withdrew to form the African Methodist Episcopal Zion Church. Prior to the split the Negro members of the church had suffered numerous and increasing embarrassments on account of their race: ". . . as the Negro membership grew in number, education, spirit, and independence, the color line was introduced. Negroes were assigned pews in the rear marked 'B. M.,' meaning black members,

[13] *Ibid.,* p. 15.

and there were discriminations at communion and baptismal font."[14]

Numerous incidents have been recorded which show that the so-called spontaneous and voluntary withdrawal of the Negroes to form their own churches was actually compelled by the discriminations and the subordinations which the Negroes suffered from white Christians in the integrated churches. The case of Richard Allen, pulled from his knees during prayer and bodily expelled from the St. George Church in Philadelphia; the special partitions and galleries for worshipers of the Negro race; segregation in the time of worship for the different races where the same building had to be used by both; the attitude of official church bodies such as that one pronounced in New York as late as 1854: "Society is unfortunately divided into classes—the intelligent, refined and elevated, in tone and character, and the ignorant, coarse and debased . . . it would seem inexpedient . . . to endeavor to compel the one class to associate on equal terms in the consultations on the affairs of the Diocese, with those whom they would not admit to their tables, or into their family circles—nay, whom they would not admit into their pews, during public worship"[15];—such moods on the part of white worshipers, such acts and incidents which were many times duplicated, are proof enough that segregation and discrimination against the Negro had been established as patterns within the Christian churches before the Negro and white churches became separate bodies and long before segregation was adopted and applied as a specific and legalized form in secular society. Nowhere does the sinful countenance of the church show so clearly its ugly features as in these early and continued denials of full fellowship to Negro Christians.

To be sure, under the circumstances nothing could have been more fortunate for the Negro than the establishing of the Negro church. The separated church became the center around which the

[14] Roi Ottley, *Black Odyssey*, Charles Scribner's Sons, New York, 1948, p. 88.

[15] Trevor Bowen, *Divine White Right*, Harper & Brothers, New York, 1934, p. 98.

Negro found his solidarity; it became the school in which Negro leadership was trained and developed; it became his refuge and shelter from the otherwise constant hammerings of an indifferent and hostile white society; it became the source of power, inspiring him toward the full expression of his humanity and undergirding his claims for a complete integration in American life with an inflexible conviction of divine approval; it became his first and fundamental social institution, antedating, as DuBois said, "by many decades the monogamic Negro home." The Negro church stands as the symbol of the white Christian's shame; yet it is a tribute to the power of the Gospel and to the faith of the Negro. West Turner, an ex-slave, said to an interviewer, "Dey law us out of church, but dey couldn't law 'way Christ."[16]

No part of the ancient wrong of the church in regard to the Negro continues so universally and so tenaciously today as does the segregation of the races in the worship of the same God and the service of the same Lord. We shall consider later and in some detail what is involved as we seek to remove this stigma; but for the moment we must merely stress the fact that what began in the church and in the secular social structure as a pattern of racial segregation threatens to continue in the church long after it has died elsewhere. The case is plain; until the middle of the second decade of this century the major denominations of the church did not officially rebuke themselves for their division of the body of Christ along racial lines. During the thirties only the Congregational Church and the Northern (American) Baptist Convention, among the larger denominations, officially condemned all forms of segregation. By the time of the Second World War the Evangelical and Reformed Church and the Presbyterians (Northern) had joined in the denunciation of segregation. And it was as late as 1946 that the Federal Council of the Churches of Christ renounced the pattern of segregation in race relations "as unnecessary and undesirable and a violation of the Gospel of love and human brother-

[16] *The Negro in Virginia*, p. 110.

hood." We have come so far in our racial thinking in the past decade that it is already difficult to appreciate the impact which this Federal Council pronouncement made upon the churches and also upon secular institutions so short a time ago. What is now a commonplace statement of Christian principle reiterated by all denominational organs was then considered a radical and daring declaration for an official arm of the Christian church.

Yet today, despite the fact that there is "scarcely a major denomination that has not declared itself in favor of integration," there has been little actual desegregation in the Protestant churches in America. Quantitatively, the record of the Roman Catholic Church with its power to outlaw segregation in its schools and churches by episcopal edict, despite the reluctance and resistance of its laymen, has been considerably better than the record of most Protestant denominations, and we must ask at the proper time what is implied by these contrasting records. To be sure there are a number of interracial churches to which Christians point with wonder, with pride, and, sometimes, with misgivings. But in the main such integration as has taken place thus far in Protestant American Christianity has fallen into one or more of the following limited patterns: (1) situations in New England and the upper Midwest where the Negro population is small and of a relatively high cultural order and where the presence of one or two Negro families has meant the difference between an exclusive and an inclusive church; (2) situations in large cities or academic centers where there is available a sufficient population of intellectual, social, and religious liberals to sustain an interracial church; (3) integration from the top, beginning with official church pronouncements and continuing with the appointment of Negroes to official boards and staff positions but not reaching down to the local church; (4) integration on the fringes, beginning with such church-related organizations as the American Bible Society, the World and National Councils of Churches, the Y.M. and Y.W.C.A., and, locally, on the edges of the church in such groups as the Boy Scouts of America, the Girl Scouts, the United Church

Women, the Inter-church Athletic Leagues, etc., yet never entering the core of the real church; (5) integration in communities in transitions where the Negro population is growing and the white population is rapidly diminishing and where the interracial church will by all practical definition soon become a Negro church attended by a few remaining whites; (6) a few churches which were deliberately organized to attract and serve a racially mixed constituency. In a word, there is little evidence that the local white churches are as yet taking seriously the resolutions and pronouncements of their respective official bodies. There are areas of the country in which this condition may change rapidly in the next decade, but there are also areas where the segregation of Negroes from the white churches will survive long after the public schools have been completely desegregated and will then die a slow and painful death. We shall meet this problem once more when we examine more closely the question of the integration of Negroes and whites in the Protestant churches. Meanwhile we know that for many years to come we shall not have to ask what is the major disgrace of the Christian church in America.

2.

Purveyor of Arrant Sedatives

Surely the wrath of men shall praise thee;
the residue of wrath thou wilt gird upon thee.
—PSALM 76:10

To suggest that religion can be used to make an oppressed people contented in their oppression or to record the fact that attempts have been made to employ Christianity for that purpose is not necessarily to reaffirm the Marxist contention that religion is the opium of the people. In the Marxist view this is the character of all religions in all ages; here we are saying that to take Christianity or any religion dedicated in principle to the full stature and whole domain of all men and to use that religion to destroy the self-respect of a particular people and to hold them at a level of subjection to other men is to profane it. In the Marxist view Christianity is being true to itself when it lulls a people who are suffering racial or economic exploitation; in our view, when Christianity is so used, it is made to contradict itself. What we are to see now is that Christianity has been so profaned in the relationship of the white Christian church and white Christians to the Negro.

34

An illustration from the ante-bellum history of South Carolina will serve to demonstrate the manner in which religion has been used by Christian people in attempts to pacify and subdue the Negro. We select this regional declaration of the value of religion as an instrument of subjection because of its historical importance and because it expressed with a candor seldom found elsewhere that desecration of religion which is more carefully concealed in other times and places. In 1829, after the invention of the cotton gin had revitalized the institution of slavery, Charles Cotesworth Pinckney, nephew and namesake of the more famous Pinckney, made a significant address before the Agricultural Society of South Carolina. The date of that address, August 18, 1829, marked the beginning of a vigorous campaign for the evangelizing of the Negro, a campaign which was to grow in intensity and not to end until the close of the Civil War thirty-five years later. In his address to his peers the aristocratic Pinckney suggested that imparting religious instructions to the slaves and securing their conversion to Christianity would serve two purposes, both profitable to the planters. First, such a program would assuage the smartings which the sensitive Southerners were feeling from Northern condemnations of slavery and might even pull the string of the Abolitionists themselves. He said, "Such a state of moral culture would give us the advantage in argument over our Northern Brethren, whose numbers and principles are respectable, and whose objection to our system is partly grounded on the deficiency of religious instruction. Were this more generally diffused, our national character would be relieved from its only real opprobrium."[1]

Second, Pinckney suggested that the imparting of Christianity to the Negro would tend to make a more docile, obedient, and tractable slave, adding moral suasion to statute and the lash as a control over the Negro. In this regard he said:

Nothing is better calculated to render man satisfied with his destiny in this world, than a conviction its hardships and trials are as transitory

[1] Susan Markey Fickling, *Slave Conversion in South Carolina 1830–1860*, University of South Carolina Press, Columbia, 1924, p. 14.

as its honors and enjoyments; and that good conduct, founded on Christian principles, will ensure superior rewards in that which is future and eternal. A firm persuasion that it is both our interest and our duty to afford religious instruction to the blacks, induces me to dwell on this subject. . . . Were true religion propagated among this numerous and important class, a sense of duty would counteract their reluctance to labor, and, diminishing the cases of feigned sickness so harassing to the Planter, would augment their numerical force and consequent production. The social relations of life being better observed, a greater proportion of domestic happiness would prevail, and render them more contented with their situation, and more anxious to promote their owner's welfare. The absence or diminution of theft, falsehood, and many other vices, would render the home of the Agriculturist far more agreeable than it can be, where guilt, which escapes human detection, knows not, and fears not, another tribunal.[2]

Seldom in the history of man has simony been proposed with so much gentility! It would be unpardonable, of course, to attribute such motives to religious activities; but when such motives are openly confessed, we must learn what we can from the confession.

That this strategy appealed to the planters of South Carolina and of the neighboring states is partly borne out by the fact that immediately afterwards there was a flourishing of sermons and articles on the duty of masters to give moral and religious instruction to their slaves. "By 1840 practically all denominations were carrying on at some point active, aggressive work among the negroes."[3] The rate of conversion among the Negroes rose sharply after 1830 and continued to rise until the collapse of the Confederacy brought a sudden end to the slave system. It would be grossly unfair to say that the Christian had no genuine interest in the moral and spiritual welfare of the Negro and that he was entirely utilitarian in his religious mission to his slaves. But it has to be concluded that the thirty-five-year period from 1830 to 1865, the period of intensified concern for the souls of the Negroes, was one in which for men of wealth and influence the economic interest was primary and the religious interest merely auxiliary. Signifi-

[2] *Ibid.*, pp. 12–13.
[3] *Ibid.*, p. 20.

cantly, Susan Fickling ends her study of slave conversion in South Carolina with these words: "However that may be, it must be admitted that the people of South Carolina before the Confederate War were evangelizing the negro only from economic and religious motives."[4] For thirty-five years "that most luscious of all combinations—religion and dividends"[5] was frankly endorsed and openly promoted.

We know that this strategy recoiled upon the planters and upon the whole system of slavery, giving the planters and their children cause to repent of their "virtues." A master who wants to keep his slave as a beast of burden must not hold before that slave a mirror in which the slave can see himself as a man. The Christian Gospel, by which the masters sought to tighten their hold upon their slaves, proved to be that kind of mirror. The Negro, looking into it, began to see himself, not as a contented, manageable slave destined to serve a superior white man, but as a person having the dignities and the rights of all God's children. In the middle decades of the nineteenth century the Negro made claim to that status but not often in open rebellion—the abortive and somewhat quixotic revolt led by Denmark Vesey in Charleston, South Carolina, in 1822, had shown the Negro the folly of throwing his limited physical powers against the preponderant force which could be mustered by the white man. He made his claim rather in songs which couched an earthly hope in vague celestial terms; in stealthy disloyalties which his master attributed to indolence, ignorance, and natural perversity; in fortifying himself inwardly for the "great day coming bye and bye"; and, whenever he could, in taking to his heels, hiding in swamp and field by day and following the North Star by night.

Moreover, that baleful history in which the white man subverted religion to economy had a second unintentional benefit for the Negro. The evangelizing of the Negro was supposed to per-

[4] *Ibid.*, p. 51.
[5] David L. Cohn, *Where I Was Born and Raised*, Houghton Mifflin Company, Boston, 1948, p. 10.

petuate him in slavery; instead it prepared him for his days of freedom. It can be and is argued by some that the Negro in 1865 was not ready for freedom; but the religious training which he had received from his master, whatever its purpose, proved to be the best possible preparation for the rigors of liberty. Bad as the days of Reconstruction were, they could have been much worse than they were for Negroes as well as whites; and it is partly owing to the religious training of the Negro that the South, coming as it did in Reconstruction to the brink of anarchy, did not plunge into complete disorder. Moreover, as we mention the unintentional by-products of the intensified converting of Negroes to Christianity, we must note that the Negro after 1877 had many of his temporal hopes blighted. He was returned to a form of peonage which differed from slavery only in technicalities. Deserted by a previously solicitous North, bereft of all power, dependent upon the mercies of a preoccupied white South, he was thrown back upon his own spiritual resources. Had there been no such spiritual resources in the time of his greatest need, the accomplishments which the Negro is now experiencing would have been still further postponed. Obviously, these facts do not exonerate the planters or excuse their profaning of religion; but they do indicate that there is a power of righteousness working in the world to turn our evil and our folly into good.

What was directly suggested by Pinckney in South Carolina in 1829 is now being discreetly proposed and systematically applied in South Africa. It is the opinion of the government of the Union of South Africa that the Christian religion can and should be used to repress and soften the intractable Bantu and to delay the time when he makes his whole claim for his whole right as a human being. The State Information Office in Pretoria, South Africa, recently released this statement:

The greatest and most difficult problem confronting the Commission was the fact that it appeared as if all efforts in connection with the development of the Bantu Areas were arrested by the unwillingness of the Bantu. How to convert this reluctance into spontaneous and purposeful action is the central problem. The question which the Commission put to itself was: Can the Christian Religion and Education perhaps achieve this? The replies bear witness to the fact that the Christian Religion is indeed a miraculous power which has radically affected the lives of the Bantu. . . . Good mission policy is good Government policy in South Africa, and forms the basis of a sound racial policy.[6]

Those who know the earlier experiment could warn the South African officials that they have ventured upon what is from their view a dangerous policy. One and the same Gospel will not forever comfort one people in their claim to superiority and content another people in their status of oppression and servitude.

The debauching of religion to dulcify an abused people, the use of Christian virtues to restrain the Negro from within while he continues to be oppressed from without, is, of course, much more subtle in our time and land than it was in the nineteenth-century Carolinas or is in South Africa; yet there is plentiful evidence that we are still willing, "without scruple of conscience," to turn religion to our profit, to use it as an instrument by which to continue the Negro in a state of subjection, and to hope that the Christian virtues of love, duty, patience, and forbearance may serve in the Negro to soften and delay his protest and his rebellion.

In vast areas of the country freedom of religion is still offered to the Negro only within limitations. The role of the Negro church, despite such significant exceptions as that one led by Martin Luther King, is still often one which bears close resemblance to the role of Judaism under the domination and tolerance of the Roman Empire. No edict is necessary; the setting itself in many sly and whispered voices says to the Negro church, "You may have your religious freedom and with it the good wishes of your white Christian brethren and the support, after a fashion, of the white community; but, in exchange, you must pay tribute to Caesar. Sing your songs; pray and preach and shout 'Amen' to your

[6] From the preface to "The Pattern of Race Policy in South Africa," *Digest of South African Affairs*, April, 1956, issued by State Information Office, Pretoria, South Africa.

hearts' content; practice your religion in freedom; but let it attend to things spiritual, future, and celestial." So, any application of the Gospel which rebukes or threatens the social structure, which carries an earthly implication, which speaks of equality in anything other than nebulous spiritual terms, which claims now the human dignities and will not wait for "the sweet bye and bye" is met by a threatened or an actual withdrawal of the patronage which is a large part of the subsistence of the Negro church in such areas. Richard Wright's story "Fire and Cloud"[7] may be fictional and somewhat out of date but it does not exaggerate the extent to which many Negro churches in the South are still beholden to, dependent upon, and abashed by the good graces of the white Christian community.

The pressures which such a setting places upon the Negro ministers and the tensions which it creates within them are titanic. It is a remarkable testimony to their stability of character and to their faith that most of them are able to maintain their outward poise and steer as successfully as they do through such diverse and contending forces. The Negro minister is immersed in external circumstances which tempt him to be an Uncle Tom; but he is also inwardly baptized with the urge to be a Moses. In a moment he must decide and keep on deciding whether the short-term gains procured by acquiescence are better than the long adventure. Being human, he is likely either to exaggerate the importance of the minor racial advances made by compromise or to conclude in passion that discretion is no part of valor. Upon him, upon the Negro minister as upon no other leader of his people, falls the almost impossible task of combining in one person the sagacity of Booker T. Washington and the temerity of Frederick Douglass.

Contrasted with his people, the Negro minister occupies a preferred status among the whites. He gets his name and perhaps even his picture in the local newspaper and his name is sometimes dignified with a title. He has his turn among the ministers of the

[7] Richard Wright, *Uncle Tom's Children,* Harper & Brothers, 1936.

community at giving devotionals over radio and television. If he come hat in hand, he is *persona grata* in the business houses where he may make a plea for white support to some charitable fund for his people or for the repair or the erecting of a place of worship. His choir may even be invited to sing in a white church, introduced by him. But he knows, if he is wise, that these perquisites are not given to him personally, that they are not evidences that he, at least, is breaking the barriers of racial segregation. He knows, or senses, the complicated, entangled motives which prompt his benefactors. Those mixed motives certainly include a genuine element of Christian compassion on the part of many white people. But they also include the white man's sense of *noblesse oblige;* and they include, openly or skillfully concealed, the white man's expectation that the Negro minister will not himself be a troublemaker but in a time of crisis will exercise a firm Christian restraint over his people. The Negro minister is expected by white people and by some Negroes to be the liaison between the white community and the black community and the palliative for an incensed and troublesome Negro people.

This use of religion to pacify the Negro in his role of secondary citizenship evolves in many subtleties which affect the moral codes of Negroes and whites. The white man for a purpose and the Negro by absorption have both accepted a double code of morality: a code for whites and a code for Negroes. Consider, for example, what the white man means by the phrase *a good Negro.* The word *good* when used by the white man as a prefix before the word *Negro* does not refer to morality in the usual sense. Indeed, a "good Negro" may be plainly, even notoriously, immoral and still in the mind of the white man deserve the title *good.* The white man will wink at the Negro's sexual frivolities so long as the Negro's promiscuity is confined to the members of his own race; he will deal a lenient judgment against the Negro who breaks the law through violence against another Negro; he will pardon truancy, petty theft, and rowdyism if they are restricted to "nigger town"; and upon such offenders against society he may still confer the appellation *good.* The white man is heard to say, "John Henry steals; he's lazy; he beats his wife; but he's a good Negro." The white woman will say of her maid or cook, "I know she's stealing me blind to feed her illegitimate children; but I can't fire her; she's so good." Obviously, in such sayings the word *good* does not refer either to efficiency or to morality; what, then, is "a good Negro?"

In the definition of the white man "a good Negro" is an in-offensive Negro; he "knows his place"; he has a built-in and un-varying sense of racial etiquette. If he is too much abused, he may protest; but his protest has the timbre of a whine and never the tone of defiance. "A good Negro" is humble, modest, deferen-tial in the presence of white people; "a bad Negro" is "uppity," forward, self-respecting and self-assertive. In other words, the atti-tude which the Negro has and shows toward the white man deter-mines whether he is worthy of the title—not his own personal morality. "A good Negro" is "a white man's Negro." It is easy and correct to conclude that the white man's definition of goodness as it pertains to the Negro has a demoralizing effect upon the Negro and, of course, upon the white man as well. We shall deal later with the demoralizing results which this double standard has upon the white man; at this point we are seeing that the white man when he preaches "goodness" to the Negro is not requiring a high, personal morality but rather demanding of the Negro that he continue to be a docile and contented serving class in American society.

What happens is that the white man cleaves Christian piety into two parts: the strong, virile virtues he applies exclusively to himself; the apparently weak, passive virtues he endorses espe-cially for the Negro. "Whatsoever things are true, honest, just, pure, lovely" belong to the white man; "whatsoever things are of good report" belong to the Negro. The white man takes the active and positive Christian adjectives for himself: noble, manly, wise, strong, courageous; he recommends the passive and negative Christian adjectives to the Negro: patient, long-suffering, humble, self-effacing, considerate, submissive, childlike, meek. It is easy for the white man to think of a Negro as a Christian; but it is difficult, if not impossible, for the white man to think of a Negro in terms of that still choice phrase, *a Christian gentleman.* This is not to say that the white man does not practice the gentle, the feminine as well as the masculine, Christian virtues; it is to say that he desires in the Negro, not a perfect and complete humanity embracing all the Christian virtues, but a limited humanity which includes only those virtues which will keep the Negro docile and tractable in a subservient social role. The Christian white man, indeed, is willing to exercise his whole Christian piety toward the Negro, with one exception: he is unwilling to grant a total Christian piety to the Negro.

The dangers involved in such a division of the Christian virtues are both fine and gross; but the danger with which we are here concerned should be immediately obvious. A cultural setting which reserves the supposedly virile virtues for one segment of the people and the passive virtues for the other segment of the people, which encourages whites to be noble, manly, and courageous and requires of Negroes that they be lowly and long-suffering, has in it the ingredients of a master-slave society. It implies that some were born to own and to rule and that others were born to serve and to be ruled; it strengthens the hold of that group which is dominant and weakens the protest of that group which is oppressed.

But we need to note further that such uses of religion are not exclusive with the South; border and Northern communities have a less obvious case of the same disease. For example, the degree to which the Negro church and the Negro minister are dependent upon the support of the white community will largely determine the extent to which the Negro church acquiesces in patterns of racial discrimination and segregation or voices a strong and effective protest, whether North or South. For example, a white church which this writer served in a Northern state owned outright the property used by a near-by and larger Negro church, renting the ground and building to the Negro church yearly for a nominal sum. The white church did not at any time interfere in the internal affairs of the Negro church; but the power implicit in ownership mitigated the racial protests which should have been made by that particular Negro community.

This much is certain: the Northern white Christian is frequently surprised when the Negro Christian aggressively demands that the rights of his people be satisfied. He, the white Christian, is puzzled when the Negro Christian insists upon moving into a white community, or uses legal instruments to secure his legal rights, or visits a white church where he is obviously not wanted, or embarrasses a genteel, white, captive audience by reciting the offenses which the white man has committed against the Negro. "How," asks the white man, "can the Negro do such things if he is really Christian—forcing himself upon other people, embarrassing his Christian brothers, causing a lot of unnecessary trouble?" And in the asking the white Christian has revealed his expectation that Christian virtues should make the Negro contented, docile, and inoffensive. His sad conclusion is, "What's the use of their being Christian if it doesn't make them leave us alone?"

A pure and complete desecration of Christianity, one in which there is not a modicum of genuine Christian compassion and sincerity, would require for its success more art and guile than most people can muster and is therefore rare. What is common, however, is the notion that religion, ours and the other person's, should somehow be made to accrue to our benefit. We bring this assumption to our interracial relationships, hoping to find in the Christian Negro one whose passions for justice have been so tempered by Christian love that he is no longer a threat to those systems of inequality which deprive him and favor us. We hope that a Christian patience will make him satisfied with interminable programs of gradualism through which he never quite reaches his full status as a man among men and a child of God but in which we can make our comfortable adjustments to whatever changes may take place. We hope that religion will make him content

44

with the simple things of life, leaving the finer things to a "superior people" who can appreciate them. We hope, in a word, that where the lash and the law no longer subject the Negro to a minor role in American life, religion will now succeed. When the Negro Christian does not follow the logic of white thought, when he does what we think that he as a Christian should not do, when he seeks his full rights, using all the instruments which the law permits and the sociological and economic and political situations provide, then we are quick to say, not that the Gospel has borne its fruits in him, but rather that he has fallen under the subverting influence of some doctrine alien to American life

This, however, is an exact opposite to the truth. The charge, hard as it is, has to be accepted: white Christians who employ Christianity to tame the protesting Negro, to keep him a partial man, to perpetuate his servile role in American society, are justifying, however unwittingly, the Marxists contention that religion is the opiate by which the exploited are appeased. And, on the other hand, Negro Christians who will not be deceived, who insist upon their full humanity, whose religion itself requires that they respect themselves as a part of sacred life and that they be complete rather than partial persons, have the honor of denying the Marxist denunciation of all religion. The escape of the Negro from those gossamer coils of spiritual passivity which the white man substituted when the physical chains were breaking and the part which the Negro's Christian faith played in discerning and breaking the almost invisible webs of spiritual enslavement should be hailed by all Christians as evidence of the powers of the Christian religion. If we who are white Christians had succeeded in pacifying the Negro through the application of soothing Christian balms, we should thereby have revealed the tragedy and the poverty of all who trust in the name of Christ. Our failure is an unexpected and extraordinary tribute to the faith which we profess and in that failure we have consolation.

What we learn from this brief analysis is that the profaning of religion for purposes of oppression and exploitation has its subtle, current forms as well as an old and open expression. We learn that the white man is not above using his religion for purposes which violate the principles of that religion; we learn that this is a strategy which recoils upon all who use it and that the Christian religion, to use again the words from South Africa, "is indeed a miraculous power" but that this miraculous power is evident, not in the control which it gives the white man over the Negro, but rather in the dignifying and liberating influence it has had in the lives of all people.

3.

Teacher of Immoral Moralities

. . . they practise fastidiousness, and imagine they are being holy.

—SCHECHTER

Christ is not the Convention, He is the Truth.

—TERTULLIAN

In one of the most penetrating sociological studies of our generation the psychologist Erich Fromm has reminded us of the fact that we customarily identify degrees of sanity and insanity by the extent to which the individual conforms to or deviates from normal social behavior. He then asks whether it is not possible that the norms of society, the standards by which we do our testing, are themselves abnormal. Is it not possible, he argues, that society itself is insane and that we therefore need a "pathology of normalcy"?[1] For our purposes it is instructive to address a similar question to our moral codes of interpersonal

[1] Erich Fromm, *The Sane Society,* Rinehart and Company, Inc., New York, 1955, p. 6.

47

relationships, particularly to those codes which govern our relations to the Negro. We must ask whether our morality is itself immoral, whether our codes of righteousness are, when applied to the Negro, a violation and distortion of the Christian ethic. Do we not judge what is right and what is wrong in racial relationships by a righteousness which is itself unrighteous, by codes and creeds which are themselves immoral?

If this should prove to be true, it would be neither a new nor a strange development in the human experience. Over his long and troubled history man's gravest sins have been, not the doing of that which is immoral, but rather the enshrining of that which is immoral as the highest morality. This was the primary problem faced by the Hebrew prophets. It was for this that Jesus came preaching that the righteousness of his time was itself unrighteous. And this, too, was a major factor in the charges which the Reformers brought against the church. Every generation needs to ask itself in what subtle way it is guilty of blasphemy and idolatry; in what way it operates, in Luther's phrase, by a "diseased law"; in what way its righteousness is unrighteous; and to what extent the church profanes its own Gospel. These are questions which the whole church and all Christian people should continually put to themselves. We are now directing such questions to the specific area described by the relationship of white Christians and Negroes and are asking whether the criteria of contemporary Christian morality are reliable in this particular area of human relationships.

We are dealing, to be sure, with a matter which is tenuous and difficult to demonstrate; but we can begin by recalling the profane uses to which the white man has put his religion in order to pacify the Negro in a subservient role in the American social order. We noted earlier two facts: first, that the white man has been guilty of using the Christian religion to make the Negro contented in his oppression, and second, that in doing so the white man has taught a double morality, reserving some of the Christian virtues exclusively for himself and recommending the passive and submissive Christian virtues especially for the Negro. That this is an immoral use of morality, a use of religion which profanes the principles of that religion, needs no further argument. But this is only a part of that complex procedure by which the white man has contaminated his code of Christian ethics and confused those standards by which he judges the righteousness of his attitudes and his behavior in dealing with members of the Negro community. We must now note in addition to the above-mentioned corruptions of religion three developments which have seriously impaired the white Christian's ability to know what is right and just in his relationship to the Negro.

In the first place we shall merely mention the well-known, much-worked, and truthful charge that Christians are skilled in isolating their sense of morality from specific areas of life and in ignoring those requirements of their moral code which are difficult to practice. This is a field thoroughly gleaned and we need only to refer to common knowledge and apply that knowledge to the relationship of white Christians to Negroes. We shall then note at some length how the white man's code of Christian morality has been diluted by the addition of concepts of gentility which are extraneous to the Christian ethic. And, in the third place, we shall consider the role that secular tradition has played in forming current concepts of Christian morality. Since the impact of gentility and tradition upon our code of morality is the more abstruse aspect of the problem and since this is a facet of racial oppression which has received too little attention, we shall spend considerable time in this area.

If, as we have already seen, the white man desecrated his religion by making it an instrument to content and perpetuate the Negro at a servile level of life and in doing so perfected a double and self-contradictory morality, he has also distorted and weakened his Christian ethic by exempting from its survey specific areas of life and by eliminating from his morality those harder demands which apply to a people who are unacceptable as neighbors, friends, and fellow Christians because of their color. Man's propensity for an easy, other-worldly Gospel which concentrates upon personal pietism and ignores the social problems has been well demonstrated in the relationship of Christians to most social injustices. It needs only to be said here that in regard to the racial problem, as also to the other social issues, the white man has restricted the scope of his moral responsibility to members of his own race and reduced the intensity of his ethic to a strictly personal pietism which ignores Christian responsibility for the Negro.

There is an eternal struggle in the heart of the enlightened Christian in regard to his relationship to the Negro. That part of him which knows the Negro as a fellow human being, made also in the image of God and due the rights and dignities which belong to all men, wrestles perpetually with that part of his soul which considers the exclusion of the Negro essential to religious propriety and cherished custom. From the stresses and strains of such an intolerable division of self against self he is tempted to take refuge in a compensatory personal piety. It may not, for example, be entirely coincidental that in America as in the Union of South Africa the extremes of pietism and racial discrimination occupy the same territory. Or, the distressed Christian substitutes for social justice a lavish and sentimental charity which always falls short of justice and which therefore never fulfills the requirements of love. In such a setting the Christian develops blind spots. For example, in his private dealings with the Negro he may display genuine compassion and charity but nevertheless be unwilling to or incapable of bringing even a verbal reproach, to say nothing of legal or social pressure, upon those social patterns which keep the Negro a continuing object of compassion and charity. He develops to the point of an art his ability to keep his religion in one pocket and the racial problems in another. We have in these words added nothing to our understanding of the racial problem but we have stressed the fact that the Christian's general reluctance to translate his ideals into practice is particularly evident in his treatment of the Negro.

Let us consider now how Christian concepts of morality have been diluted by the inclusion of notions of propriety and decorum which are not essential to and which in many cases contradict Christian principles of human relationships. It will be helpful, once more, to begin in the distant past and then bring the force of this thought to bear upon our present attitudes toward members of the Negro society. Quite early in the history of American slavery morals and manners became synonymous; and the manners which debased and ostracized the Negro triumphed over the morals which should have honored and embraced him as a fellow human being. Indeed, even before slavery had become a legalized institution, there had developed a code of morality which justified the debasing of the Negro to a subhuman level, which drove a wedge of "righteousness" between whites and blacks, and which gave divine sanction to a rigid separation of the races. "As early as 1630 the conduct of a white man who had violated a rule of strict (sexual) segregation of the white and black races was denounced as an 'abuse to the dishonor of God and shame of Christians,' and in atonement for such conduct the white man received a sound whipping and was required to make public apology."[2] The conduct cited was reprehensible for its own demerit; the point, however, is that the sin was considered compounded by the fact that it was interracial. This describes a developing mood and ". . . before the end of the 17th century many of the white colonists came to regard them [Negroes] as not of human kind."[3]

Through the following years this contempt for the personality of the Negro had in every decade an official endorsement from some representative of the Christian church, employing in the main Biblical arguments to prove the native inferiority of Negroes and their ordination as "hewers of wood and drawers of water." In our own time members of the clergy who preach racist doctrines, who join White Citizens Councils, who obstruct justice for the

[2] John H. Russell, *The Free Negro in Virginia, 1619–1865,* Johns Hopkins University Studies, Vol. 31, Baltimore, 1913, p. 123.
[3] *Ibid.,* p. 124.

Negro or for any other minority are not generally held in respect by their fellow members of the clergy; and it must be noted for the record that the Christian ministry in the South is in the main keenly aware of the depth and the scope of the racial problem and, all things considered, is more courageous and forthright in its actions and declarations than is expected. But the long years in which the church gave official sanction to the subjection of the Negro and attributed divine approval to the strictest segregation of the races have done a work which will not quickly be undone. Under the impact of such preachments and by a natural desire to rationalize and justify the mistreatment of the Negro the racial attitude of white people became a part of their religion, a major and unwritten doctrine of their moral code. A deeply imbedded sense of propriety which required the segregation of the Negro became fixed not only in the code but also in the moral consciousness of white Christians.

If we are to see clearly how morality and gentility became synonymous and the effects of this blending, we must see these developments first where they are dramatically presented. We can say that the Southern Christian is in general the most pietistic religionist in the land, the word *pietistic* being used now in its fine, true, and complimentary sense. He takes his religion seriously; his church life is his pride and his joy. His moral code is earnestly held and is as conscientiously practiced as is that of any fallible human being. The charges by outsiders that he "does not live his religion" are either unjust, hypocritical, or false. To be sure, he habitually defaults his Christianity in one of the major and important areas of human relationships, but this is characteristic of Christians generally and does not nullify his whole Christian life. And it is, indeed, precisely here that our interest focuses. He sees his racial behavior, not as a default, but rather as a faithful performance of his Christian ethic. So this intense and extensive self-awareness of religion in the South is cited, not as an apology for the white South, but rather to stress the fact that the Southerner's concept of morality, by a long history of distortion, has become a block to his acceptance of racial integration. It requires, on the one hand, that he be benevolent, indulgent, paternalistic toward the Negro; but that same morality requires also that he strictly avoid any of those relationships with the Negro which are proscribed by the conventions of his people and which are, in his opinion, frowned upon by his God. Deep in the fibers of his soul there is the fear that shaking a Negro's hand, tipping his hat to a Negro woman, sitting at meal with colored people, swimming with them in the same pool, admitting them to his church, may be a mortal sin, "an abuse to the dishonor of God and shame of Christians."

What has happened here is that religion and gentility have become inseparable. In the South the accent upon breeding, good taste, propriety, refinement has been strong in the middle and upper classes and even among that segment of the very poor which feels itself different from and infinitely superior to "poor white trash." The words *lady* and *gentleman* imply an awareness of that which is fitting and proper, a sense of discretion, an appreciation of values. Even among the very poor, children are often taught pride of ancestry and of person, of blood and breeding. It would be a mistake to write off this custom as a cultural vestige inherited from the South's aristocratic past or to find it completely deplorable. Its merits are, in fact, more obvious than its demerits. But as the accents upon nobility, propriety, and decorum grew heavier and heavier, gentility was driven deep into the realm of religion and the two became in most minds identical. The rule reads: to be morally correct one must be genteel; to be right one must be proper; to be a Christian one must be a lady or a gentleman.

The tragedy of Southern gentility, so far as the racial problem is concerned, is that it included classified human beings in the catalogue of those things to be properly avoided by a gentle Christian people. The standards of gentility, of quality, assumed that no self-respecting person would enter into personal associations with Negroes, Croatans, Lumbees, mulattoes—whatever their cultural

level—or with the "poor white trash" who did so, however innocent and innocuous those same associations might be between
people of the same class and color. The prohibitions, it must be
remembered, were not merely a part of social etiquette but even
more were fraught with concepts and emotions of righteousness.
Gentility, moreover, in its august moral tones, drove its cleaver
not merely between peoples who were culturally and morally dissimilar but also between peoples who were culturally and morally
identical and only racially dissimilar. It was assumed—errone-
ously—that the most intimate of all physical and illicit relationships between the races took place only between the dregs of the
white and Negro social orders. Therefore, on the basis of that
fallacious assumption it was concluded that the more distance a
respectable white person could put between himself and the
Negro the more assured he was of his badge of genteel morality.
Thus a morality which by its own principles should be a hinge
reconciling people to people, irrespective of dissimilarities, became instead the wedge dividing the racial groups.

An excellent and precise illustration of the use of gentility as an
endorsement of racial oppression became a few years ago a matter
of public record and is evidence of the fact that in broad areas of
the country gentility is assumed to be a necessary ingredient of
morality. It will be recalled that the Phi Kappa Psi board had
ousted the Amherst chapter for pledging a Negro. Shortly afterwards the president of the National Interfraternity Conference,
sustaining the action of the Phi Kappa Psi board and speaking in
favor of the exclusion of Negroes, said, "I love the discriminating
tongue, the discriminating eye, and the discriminating ear, and,
above all, the discriminating mind and soul. The person for whom
I can find no love and respect is the indiscriminating person. To
be indiscriminate is to be common, to be vulgar."[4] Thus an appeal
was made to good taste to justify the rude exclusion of qualified
Negroes from fraternities. The word *discriminating,* as used here,

[4] Carey McWilliams, *Brothers Under the Skin,* Little, Brown and Company,
Boston, 1951, p. 54.

is a *double-entendre;* the delicate meaning of the word is used to defend the indelicate function of the word. What is missing from the equation is the fact that true gentility, to say nothing of Christian morality, discerns human values which transcend superficial human differences. A discriminating Christian, in other words, will not discriminate against the Negro simply because he is a Negro. His good taste may properly exclude certain undesirable Negroes and whites from the intimate circles of home and friendship. This he may do without the need for compunction. But his Christian sense of morality, if it is uncontaminated by spurious notions of propriety, will not permit and certainly should not be used to sanction the unjust exclusion of Negroes from those social areas for which they are qualified and to which they properly belong.

Questionnaires which have sought explanations of the white man's aversion to integration have elicited numerous concrete answers; but they have also uncovered a volume of replies which can only be classified as a deep-seated, mystical, religious abhorrence of social contact between Negroes and whites. Such answers are often vague, halting, and incoherent; but that fact does not indicate that the one questioned has been driven into a corner and has no further defense for his opposition to integration. On the contrary, far from being exhausted, he has merely fallen back to what is for him the strongest position of all—his impregnable conviction that association of the races on levels of equality would be immoral, "an abuse to the dishonor of God and shame of Christians." The fact that he is not articulate in expressing this conviction, the fact that he has retreated to the seemingly lame assertion, "It just isn't right," does not indicate, as it seems to, that he can now be easily dislodged from this final fortress of racial segregation. For here the centuries have stored for him an inexhaustible ammunition, and a cherished custom has ringed his core of resistance with walls which no logic can penetrate. A gentility which involves separation from the Negro has transformed itself into an unassailable religious taboo.

No one is better prepared to give testimony to this fact than is that white man who has been partially released from prejudice against the Negro. He believes himself to be a completely "reconstructed" white man. He has studied and accepted the findings of anthropology and sociology at high levels and there is no advanced and liberal theory of race relations to which he would not give mental assent. His conduct toward the Negro is a model of correctness. Then, to his consternation, his racial poise is one day shattered by moods of uneasiness which, coming from some deep internal place, thrust themselves into his consciousness and question the "rightness" of his interracial behavior. He has long ago discarded the sophistries about the racial inferiority of the Negro; he has deliberately broken the patterns of social segregation—some of his best friends are Negroes; he has no conscious desire to return to those folkways from which in some agony of soul he long ago departed; but here, in him of all people, there has appeared this strange and perplexing anxiety: his deeply imbedded religious taboo against the mixture of the races, forgotten and supposedly expelled, has re-entered its demur. It may have shrunk now to nothing more than a doubt, a suspicion, the ghost of earlier convictions about the relationship of Negroes and whites; but this apparition, unaccountably summoned from the depths of his soul, is enough to disturb his serene confidence that he, at least, has solved the problems of racial prejudice.

It is, of course, not only among Southerners that we find among Christian people this deep, mystical aversion to personal relations between Negroes and Caucasians. To be sure, the immoral morality which can be rather easily demonstrated in the attitude of the white Southerner toward the Negro is far better concealed, less extensive, and perhaps less intense north of the Mason-Dixon line. But here, too, there is a general and variously expressed suspicion that the social intermingling of Negroes and whites is practiced only by the dregs of the white community, by the poor and the ignorant, left-wing liberals, Bohemians, conniving politicians, or occasionally by the clergy and by eccentric socialites who take up race relations for a season or two as a "cause." Interracial marriage is considered immoral and in several Northern states is still outlawed; restrictive covenants, providing a sanitary cordon around exclusively white communities, are considered a proper protection for "better-class" white people; private and semipublic clubs in which membership is based upon social rank exclude all members of the Negro race whatever their cultural standing, thus declaring color an indelible mark of unacceptability; and white Christian churches, though they do not resent an occasional Negro visitor, assume hopefully that the Negro in choosing his permanent church home will prefer to be "among his own." Such devices for the segregation of the races and the maintenance of propriety do not, of course, have the official endorsement of the church in the North any more than they do in the South. But throughout the country it is assumed by the majority of Christian people that this is the right way, the moral way, the Christian way to maintain harmonious relations between the races. There are exceptions, but in general the white Christian, wherever he lives and whatever his political tradition, considers it entirely proper that his church has not entered the civic and political arena to champion the cause of the Negro. As he sees it, it is one thing to discuss what the Christian attitude should be; it is quite another thing for the church to act according to its own principles of Christian morality. In the opinion of most white Christians it is unbecoming of the white man—indeed, boorish—to follow Christian logic into action and deal with Negroes without regard to their color; and it is assumed that white Christians will hold themselves circumspectly aloof from any social contact with Negroes, which would make their morality suspect.

We can see, then, to summarize this thought, that a considerable part of the problem of race relations resides in the inability of the white man to determine where the privileges of personal preference end and where the requirements of Christian morality begin. To him a strict Christian ethic seems to require that he renounce all the standards of etiquette, manners, and propriety which a gentle and civilizing culture has taught him and which to him have become the essence of morality. It seems to require that he relinquish his rules of order, lose the taste for beauty, and abjure all elegance and refinement. In him is the perplexing but very real question: "Must I be common in order to be Christian?" Such a person, earnestly seeking some way out of the dilemma posed by an ethic which in its strictness contradicts his sense of refinement and good taste, must be taught that there is a Christian gentility transcending fashion and convention; he must be shown that good manners do not determine but are set by good morals. He must be assured that there is a place in his life where personal preference has authority but that there is also the vaster realm of life in which personal preference must be forfeited to the prior claims of the rights of other people. He must be persuaded that the genuineness of Christian morality takes priority over the gentilities of social correctness. He must learn, as Confucius put it, that "a gentleman is one who finds something scalding in the touch of evil" and that what the white man must therefore abhor if he is to be a Christian gentleman is not the touch of ignorance, poverty, disease, or the rusticities of the common people, not the touch of a different class or culture or color, but the touch of that evil by which he himself degrades and deprives and denies a fellow human being.

However superfluous the suggestion may seem to some of us, it is well to remember that many well-intentioned people are sincerely puzzled and are hampered in their human relationships because they have not distinguished or cannot distinguish between that natural love which prefers and has the right to prefer its own kind and that Christian love which has nothing to do with likes or dislikes or with kind but transcends human differences and disagreements. All preaching and teaching of the Gospel of Christian love must acknowledge, indeed must stress, the difference between the exclusiveness which filial love requires and the inclusiveness which Christian love demands. Where people are considering who will and who will not be invited as guests into their homes, whom they will accept as intimate friends and con-

fidants, whom they will marry or not marry, their own codes of
acceptability are the final authority. It is not bigotry to prefer the
company of those who share one's interests, who have similar
tastes and manners; it is not prejudice in the usual and vicious
sense of the word to seek those with whom one has natural feelings of congeniality and to avoid in personal intercourse those
whose interests and personalities clash with one's own. Jesus spent
his leisure with Martha, Mary, and Lazarus, not with Herod and
Caiaphas. Where personal friendship is concerned, there personal
and mutual preference is supreme.

This distinction has not been more fairly or clearly stated than
it was by George W. Cable, the Southern novelist, who, in "The
Silent South," an 1885 essay much beyond its time and foreign to
its New Orleans origin, wrote, "All the relations of life that go by
impersonal right are Civil relations. All that go by *personal choice*
are Social relations. The one is all of right, it makes no difference
who we are; the other is all of choice, and it makes all the difference who we are. For the one we make laws; for the other everyone consults his own pleasure; and the law that refuses to protect
a civil right, construing it a social privilege, deserves no more
regard than if it should declare some social privilege to be a
civil right."

Our error as well-intentioned white people is not that we make
such a distinction—the distinction is valid—but that we have
taken the Negro's "dues" out of the area of his civil rights, where
we should be under obligation to honor them, and put them in
the area of our social privilege, where we grant them only if we
choose to do so. We have refused "to protect a civil right, construing it a social privilege." We use our personal arguments
against social leveling to deprive the Negro of his sociological
rights. We are opposed to integration of Negroes and whites on
buses, in trains, and in schools on the basis of personal choice;
but this matter lies, not in the area of our social privilege, but in
the area of the Negro's civil rights. Some people do not want
Negroes as close friends or members of the family and construe

this personal preference as just cause for excluding Negroes from hotels, restaurants, and churches. They prefer the companionship of members of their own race and conclude that they are therefore justified in barring Negroes from those public and semipublic clubs for which Negroes are disqualified solely on account of their race. They do not want to marry him and conclude that they must therefore deny him the rights of a neighbor.

It is one thing to insist that our personal preference in matters purely social is sacred and should not be invaded; but it is grossly unfair, illogical, and unjust to reduce the Negro's civil rights to the level of social privilege so that we may trample upon both his civil rights and his personal choices as we please. If there is any validity at all in the Christian ethic, we shall have to concede, when we turn to the right of the Negro to belong, that his claim upon Christians involves something more than his civil rights; but we are saying for the moment that when our sense of good breeding and personal preference degrades and deprives the Negro in the area of his human rights then our morality is Christian only by the grossest distortion of the word.

The part which secular tradition has played in diluting our code of Christian morality closely parallels the influence of manners upon morals but has, nevertheless, made its own distinct contributions to the weakening of the Christian ethic. The influence of tradition upon morality is clearly seen in the South, where tradition is reverenced more openly than it is in other areas of the country. There tradition is sacred—sacred in the sense that it has become an integral part of religion. The religious quality of Southern tradition was referred to by Hamilton Basso, somewhat extravagantly but picturesquely, as "The Shinto Tradition of the American South."[5] This tradition remains despite all the superficial changes which are taking place in the South. The industrial changes which occur in the South today are exciting and extraor-

[5] Hamilton Basso, *The View from Pompey's Head,* Doubleday and Company, Inc., New York, 1954, p. 10.

dinary, but these changes are not evidences of the crumbling of Southern tradition. "Stark Young's assertion in 1930 that the changing South was still the South applied with equal force twenty years later. There had been, as we have seen, a great increase in the section's wealth without any great alteration in its relative economic position in the nation. There had been no social or political revolution. The South was set off from the rest of the United States by issues not much different from what they had been for the past generation or two."[6] Change at the deeper levels of life is still alien and viewed with suspicion, as though a break with tradition would be a violation of a sacred heritage, the repudiation of father and mother, the desecration of the graves of ancestors, a desertion of compatriots, and a rebuke to God.

Certainly this is not altogether bad; the powers of cohesion which are inherited in a cherished tradition can, indeed, solidify and strengthen a people; but, unhappily, this tradition has become associated with congealed and accepted concepts of and attitudes about and toward the Negro. A break with these inherited and conventional opinions on race means in the sensitive, religious patriot the pulling up of deep roots which are entwined around precious concepts of home, history, ancestry, and religion. To cut the roots of such a sanctified tradition, to break that convention which honors the segregating of the races, and to sever those strong ties of community in which personality is anchored and given stability requires a rare fortitude. The white man may assent intellectually to the charge that Negroes are grossly mistreated; but, unless he be a person of exceptional depth and maturity of character, a break with the social order and with those traditions which are essential to it courts for him a kind of psychic suicide from which he instinctively recoils. He is therefore slow to speak and slower still to move against the inherited and continuing injustices of his own racial patterns.

Although we have seen here a regional illustration of the im-

[6] Francis Butler Simkins, *A History of the South*, Alfred A. Knopf, New York, 1953, p. 597.

pact of tradition upon morality, we must remember that the traditional attitude of the white man toward the Negro has to a large degree infected the whole nation. For most of us the days preceding our birth provided the patterns of racial practice which are current in our time, and over those practices the years have thrown the aura of sanctity. We shall consider later the claims which the prevailing social climate makes upon those who are born into it; here we can say that most of us opened our eyes and our consciousness upon a social order in which racial segregation and discrimination had general approval. Such a social order, even though we may be the ones deprived by it, exercises over us a kind of sanctified parental authority.

Many years ago Reinhold Niebuhr[7] indicated how difficult, if not impossible, it is for human societies and social groups to act on the basis of a high and radical morality, stating, as we may put it, that societies are soulless and at best amoral. This was a significant and brilliantly developed idea; but what now needs to be emphasized is not merely the absence of ethical sensitivity in social groups but the ability of the individual Christian to exempt himself from all sense of personal responsibility for the actions of his group and from his own involvement in its failings and to do so on the basis of what he considers to be the prior claims of his religion and by the substituting of personal piety for social justice.

At bottom the question for the church as it faces the racial evils of our day is not whether man is moral and society immoral but whether the whole formula by which Christians test rightness and wrongness in man and in society is itself corrupt. Has the racial sickness become over the years so insidious and so epidemic in its proportions that we are tempted to construe the universality of that disease as an evidence of health? We must answer that it has. Do we not, then, need in race relations, more than anything else, a pathology of morality? We must answer that we do. The

[7] Reinhold Niebuhr, *Moral Man and Immoral Society,* Charles Scribner's Sons, New York, 1932.

church must therefore ask of itself whether it has generated, fostered, or permitted a concept of racial morality which is immoral; and to that question it must reply that it has. It must ask to what extent religion has been, not a solution, but "a potent conservator" of those white ways which abuse the Negro, and it must confess in answer that religion more than any other single influence has given racial injustice its abiding power. And it must ask what the church must do to propagate among its people and impress upon its culture the righteousness which is the will of God for all His people. We shall know, at least, the depth and tenacity of the problem, for we have seen that the religion to which we should be able to appeal for a solution of the racial tensions and divisions has become itself a producer and protector of such tensions and divisions. How shall we span the gulf between the races if the bridge itself remain a barrier?

This, done in broad strokes, is the portrait of the countenance of the church, reflected in the mirror of race. This is the story of the white Christian people and their churches in relationship to the Negroes of America. So far as the major denominations are concerned, it is the story of indifference, vacillation, and duplicity, with occasional interludes in which the church came alive to its duty only to sink after a time into renewed indifference. It is a history in which the church not only compromised its ethic to the mood and practice of the times but was itself actively unethical, sanctioning the enslavement of human beings, producing the patterns of segregation, urging upon the oppressed Negro the extracted sedatives of the Gospel, and promulgating a doctrine of interracial morality which is itself immoral. It is a story in which none of us can take either joy or pride unless we happen to be members of one of those minor cults which from the beginning voiced a protest against the evils of slavery and sought among themselves as well as in the general society the removal of those evils. It is a story in which men like Fox, Woolman, Garrison, Whittier, Channing have unusual stature partly because they stood upon such vast, dismal plains of Christian indifference and inactivity. And it is a continuing story in which many of the errors and deliberate evils of the past are firmly entrenched in the present and give warning of their intention to move with us into the future. We must recite this story and keep the general facts of it in memory, not because we want to condemn or to redeem our ancestors, but because this is a stream of human events which is flowing forcefully into our times and lives and with which we as a Christian people must reckon.

Part Two
Diagnosis by Definition

4.

The Nature of Prejudice

Reason and humanity have raised their
voices in vain—
for grey-headed prejudice is deaf.

—MOSES MENDELSSOHN

Never get rid of your soul's anxiety except
by looking unto the Lord Jesus. If you
get rid of your anxiety in any other way,
it may never return.

—McCHEYNE

In summarizing the causal factors of racial prejudice, the psychologist Gordon W. Allport writes, "There is no master key. Rather what we have at our disposal is a ring of keys, each of which opens one gate of understanding."[1] This is an important warning and corrective for those who propose single and simplified explanations of the complicated nature of prejudice. Each specialist who gives attention to the problem is tempted to see it and to find its solution in the light of his own specialty. The

[1] Gordon W. Allport, *The Nature of Prejudice,* The Beacon Press, Boston, 1954, p. 208.

educator blames ignorance and proposes education; the sociologist cites the impregnating pressures of mores, folkways, and traditions and suggests arbitrary changes in the societal systems; the historian reminds us of those insensate forces which, like the invention of the cotton gin, coerce man, willy-nilly, into prescribed patterns of thought and feeling and action, and he recommends patience; the Marxist sees racial prejudice solely as a rationale for exploitation and is confident that the equalizing of material goods among all people will prevent class and race conflict; the psychologist speaks in terms of the frustration-aggression hypothesis. Only by a compilation of the various factors productive of racial prejudice, drawing together the peculiar insights and narrow conclusions of the several specialists, do we avoid the errors, the exaggerations, and the omissions of singular speculations on the meaning of prejudice. The Christian church in its approach to the problem must be mindful of this temptation to make excessive claims for a particular point of view; but the Christian church thus far has erred, not in being categorical about its own theory, but in being eclectic in its search for explanations of racial prejudice. It is here held that an extreme and highly specialized Christian view which could be laid over against paralleling theories would contribute more to an understanding of the racial problem than do our Christian repetitions and embellishments of socio-scientific theories.

It must be noted that the social scientists, in collaboration or going their independent ways, have fashioned a versatile and competent "ring of keys." Indeed, apart from the studies made by anthropologists, psychologists, and sociologists there are no reliable data on what is without doubt the major and most serious problem of human relationships in our time. By contrast the church either in timidity or in indifference has defaulted in almost total silence. Such studies as have been made toward an understanding of the racial disorders in our society must be credited to the social sciences, and such progress as has been made toward the solving of those disorders is the merit, not of the church, but of the secular institutions in our culture. We must not, of course, as the late Dr. Charles

S. Johnson warned, indict the Christian faith because of the church's failure, nor must we forget the permeating influence of that faith upon the social sciences and the secular institutions.[2] Nevertheless, even a casual survey of the voluminous literature, which runs into thousands of volumes on the subject of race and race prejudice, and a hasty classification of the areas and agencies of progress and solution leave the church condemned and the social sciences and secular institutions highly accredited.

But as we examine this "ring of keys" provided by the social sciences to open gates of understanding, we discover about them what is from the Christian view a significant and impairing fact: they do not in any combination open and reveal the inner secrets of racial hostility. This is acknowledged even by the specialists themselves. In a work which is certainly as exhaustive and definitive as any, Gunnar Myrdal confessed that there are yet unfathomed depths in the problem of prejudice. He says:

In this magical sphere of the white man's mind, the Negro is inferior, totally independent of rational proofs or disproofs. And he is inferior in a deep and mystical sense. *The reality of his inferiority is the white man's own indubitable sensing of it, and that feeling applies to every single Negro.* This is a manifestation of the most primitive form of religion. There is fear of the unknown in this feeling, which is "superstition" in the literal sense of the word. . . . So the Negro becomes a "contrast conception." He is "the opposite race"—an inner enemy, "antithesis of character and properties of the white man." His name is the antonym of white.[3]

The varied sociological explanations of racial prejudice, however different they seem from each other when superficially observed, are found upon closer examination to have a basic similarity. It is a similarity in defect as though the keys, having all been cast in a common mold, carry with them the flaw of that mold. For

[2] Charles S. Johnson, *Into the Mainstream,* The University of North Carolina Press, Chapel Hill, 1947, p. 281.

[3] Gunnar Myrdal, *An American Dilemma,* Harper & Brothers, New York, 1944, p. 100. (Italics his.)

the plain fact is that most, if not all, sociological interpretations of racial prejudice rest upon the same erroneous assumption about the nature of man. This does not mean that such theories are therefore completely erroneous—that is obviously not true—but it does mean that all socio-psychological explanations of racial prejudice which are founded upon a false reading of the nature of man must be always somewhat in error and never complete.

The assumption upon which the social scientists and psychologists build their theories of prejudice is that prejudice is not inherent in human beings but acquired. For example, R. M. MacIver, whose *The More Perfect Union* is here highly recommended as a study of group relations, declares that most explanations of the nature of prejudice "fail to do justice to the intricately interwoven social strands in the social complex. . . . Prejudice is not the expression of the native reaction of individuals to the actual attributes of other individuals or of whole groups."[4] This has become a veritable dogma with the sociologists; it is for them an unquestioned, unquestionable, and irreducible hypothesis. It is common to all the specialists in the field, from the proponents of the frustration-aggression theory to the champions of economic determinism; and, unfortunately, it is thoughtlessly echoed by the larger part of those Christian writers who have given their attention to this theme. The seemingly conclusive and seemingly incontrovertible evidence is offered that so far as race is concerned all little children are free from racial prejudice. They say that no one is born with race prejudice, that race prejudice has to be learned, seemingly unaware of the fact that the truth of these assertions is beside the point when we are considering the origin of prejudice itself and is not clinical evidence of the innate innocence of human nature. Or, to put the matter in more erudite words, they hold with John Locke, to whom "the newborn child was a *tabula rasa* upon which the 'sensations'—that is, in modern language, the entirety of life experiences—made their imprint. Environment was made supreme

[4] R. M. MacIver, *The More Perfect Union,* The Macmillan Company, New York, 1948, p. 80.

, . apparent differences were of cultural origin, and men could be changed through education."[5]

All monolithic explanations of the nature of prejudice rise from the plain of this sociological axiom. For example, it has been held that racism is a new thing under the sun, originating not more than 150 years ago, its birth and growth being coincident with the flourishing of capitalism and its flow from country to country following in the wake of capitalism and being restricted to those countries in which the colonial dominance of the white man had been established. From this partial truth Oliver C. Cox, in a well-argued but narrow thesis, has concluded that ". . . race prejudice is the social-attitudinal concomitant of the racial-exploitative practice of a ruling class in a capitalistic society,"[6] which is his cumbersome way of saying that race prejudice is nothing more or less than a tool of capitalism. To leave no doubt about his meaning Cox said, "We have attempted to show that race prejudice is peculiar to the system of capitalistic exploitation."[7]

Cox has been joined by many interpreters who disclaim Marxist sympathies but who share the opinion that racial antagonisms are basically a rationale for discriminative economic exploitation. Even Naomi Goldstein, whose untimely death cut short a promising career in the area of racial understanding and whose penetrations of the problem were keen and deep, concluded that "the history of race ideas is a history of defense of inequality and exploitation."[8] That this is a virile and tenacious argument, uncovering many of the festering sources of racial oppression, cannot and should not be denied. Nevertheless, it leaves vast areas of racial hostility untouched; and, beyond that, so far as ultimate sources of prejudice are concerned, it is an explanation which does not explain. When prejudice is defined strictly as an unemotional device,

[5] Myrdal, *op. cit.*, p. 83.

[6] Oliver Cromwell Cox, *Caste, Class, and Race,* Doubleday and Company, Garden City, N.Y., 1948, p. 476.

[7] *Ibid.*, p. 400.

[8] Naomi Friedman Goldstein, *The Roots of Prejudice Against the Negro in the United States,* Boston University Press, Boston, 1948, p. 22.

a dispassionate tool, a useful pretense for the enslaving or exploiting of a people, what is being defined is not prejudice but duplicity. Prejudice ceases to be prejudice when it is not emotionally felt or when it ceases to be sincere. On the other hand, when prejudice is emotional and is sincerely held, it can no longer be defined as a mere instrumentality.

The direct relationship between specialized theories and the fundamental assumption that prejudice is a sociological product absorbed or adopted by the human personality is exemplified in those explanations which are interested in prejudice as a result rather than as a cause. This is the "vicious circle" theory, by which students of the problem mean that the effects of prejudice become in turn the causes of prejudice, thus forming a self-perpetuating system of racial or religious oppression. Carey McWilliams voices this position as follows: "Race relations are not based on prejudice; prejudice is a by-product of race relations—as influenced by other factors."[9] In this view discrimination and segregation are the cause and prejudice is the effect. Of course, Carey McWilliams is too able and devoted a student of racial problems to be accused of a wholesale dismissal of prejudice as a prime cause, but he does lean in the work cited and in others to the view that prejudice is often a pretense for or a result of discrimination and segregation.

In *The Mark of Oppression* by Kardiner and Ovesey we have a psychological explanation of this point of view: "Once you degrade someone in that way, the sense of guilt makes it imperative to justify the entire procedure. . . . The only defense now is to hate the object."[10] Thus patterns of discrimination and oppression become not only the nest in which the eggs of prejudice are laid and hatched but also the hen which does the laying. This is surely an incisive and helpful understanding of the origin of many of our racial antagonisms and enforces that strategy which requires a di-

[9] Carey McWilliams, *Brothers Under the Skin,* Little, Brown and Company, Boston, rev. ed., 1951, p. 315.
[10] Abraham Kardiner and Lionel Ovesey, *The Mark of Oppression,* W. W. Norton and Company, New York, 1951, p. 379.

rect assault upon all discriminatory and, therefore, demoralizing systems within our society.

Even so, the "vicious circle" theory says nothing to us about the primordial origin and nature of prejudice; and, in the main, its disciples disclaim any desire to do so. R. M. MacIver says, "The principle of the 'vicious circle' shows how group prejudice is maintained, not how it comes into being. It takes the mores of prejudice as a datum."[11] We should have to insist from the Christian standpoint that the social systems fertilize but do not generate the prejudices of man. Or we might say more accurately that racial oppression will tend to release restricted prejudices, giving them substance and form.

It might be thought that among the socio-psychological keys for opening our understanding of racial prejudice there is one which is not from the common mold and which does not carry the flaw of the others, a theory not based upon the dogma that prejudice is a sociological product. This is the theory championed by those who are interested in the psychodynamics of human relationships and in the functioning of personality. Here explanations do move closer to the Judeo-Christian understanding of the nature of man; yet in a crucial particular they remain distinct from it. In general social psychology and the Christian faith agree in their descriptions of human behavior, but they do not agree in their definition of the elemental nature of man. This is nowhere better illustrated than in two lines from the psychologist Allport. In the one he states that he has for a full chapter contended "that man has a propensity to prejudice."[12] Surely the main lines of Christian theology would not contradict this contention. Yet, in the second reference, Allport declares that ". . . personality is what it is chiefly because of the way he was socialized (training in family, school, and neighborhood)."[13] What he thus declares to be the essential nature and the

11 *Op. cit.*, p. 80.
12 *Op. cit.*, p. 27.
13 *Ibid.*, p. 208.

primary nurture of human personality Christian theology must deny.

Yet it should be stressed that between the Christian faith and social psychology there are broad areas toward which they come from opposite directions but in which they find meaningful agreement and mutual assistance. Simpson and Yinger in *Racial and Cultural Minorities,* the ablest and most complete survey of the racial field since Myrdal's *An American Dilemma,* admit as one of three basic causes that "prejudice may be partly understood as a manifestation of the 'needs' of individual personality."[14] And they add that "Prejudice may be an attempt to enhance one's self-esteem or to remove a threat to self-esteem."[15] Bruno Bettelheim and Morris Janowitz entertained four hypotheses on the dynamics of prejudice in their case histories of 150 World War II veterans, all hypotheses having to do with the functioning of personality.[16] And these citations are merely indicative of the increasing and valued interest of psychologists in the study of prejudice.

Consider for specific illustration the frustration-aggression theory which Naomi Goldstein called "the most satisfactory psychological approach to the problem of race prejudice."[17] Here, certainly, the Christian interpretation of human conduct has been influential or is implied. In digest the theory is that when we are blocked in the achieving of some personal goal, either by other people, by natural forces, or by personal inadequacy, hostile impulses are the result. This hostility can be directed toward the frustrating object, but often it cannot be so directed. The object may be an uncontrollable condition or a powerfully superior person, or a beloved "in-group" person. In this case the hostility is stored up or directed toward some substitute object which is avail-

[14] George Eaton Simpson and J. Milton Yinger, *Racial and Cultural Minorities: An Analysis of Prejudice and Discrimination,* Harper & Brothers, New York, 1953, p. 66.

[15] *Ibid.,* p. 83.

[16] Bruno Bettelheim and Morris Janowitz, *Dynamics of Prejudice,* Harper & Brothers, New York, 1950, p. 36.

[17] *Op. cit.,* p. 53.

able and unable to retaliate. Psychologically, one and the same mood makes a balked child stamp the floor, a fired laborer kick his dog, a discouraged salesman slur his wife, a gentile defame a Jew, and a white man deride a Negro. This explanation of racial prejudice, as is true of others in the psychological approach, is easily turned from psychoanalysis to Christian homiletics, so much akin are they in describing the functionings of the human personality. Even so, the fundamental disagreement between the Christian faith and the general field of psychology remains: they disagree in their definition of the essential nature of man.

Thus to the social scientists, even to the social psychologists, prejudice is not natural but artificial, not cohesive to human personality but adhesive, not indigenous but an additive which is removed by solvents found in the rearranging of some part or parts of the social order or by education. They assume, in Pascal's phrase, that human nature is "sound, needing no redeemer." They conclude, in a word, by laying the blame for racial prejudice upon everything except the essential nature of the human personality and by finding its solution everywhere except in a radical change of that essential nature.

It has been said of Nicolas Berdyaev that to him "all the doctrines of sociology are erroneous because they are based on a false estimate of man, namely as an object among other objects; as a member of society which is itself an impersonal object and a theoretical abstraction."[18] We do not agree that all the doctrines of sociology are wrong, but we do claim that those which have to do with the nature of prejudice are based on a false estimate of the nature of man and therefore cannot be complete or fundamental. The error of the sociologists is a fundamental error; they begin with a fallacious presupposition, the assumption that man, reduced to his essential self, is a social being and can therefore be explained and can only be explained by social facts.

It therefore remains for the Christian faith to accent "the full

[18] George Seaver, *Nicolas Berdyaev,* Harper & Brothers, New York, 1950, p. 73.

75

inwardness of the situation," to insist that there is a serious omission from the "ring of keys" which the social scientists offer in explanation of prejudice—the key to that inner and central room of human nature and human relationships, the soul, around which all the other rooms are but as concentric courts. More correctly, Christian theology would insist that the several keys which unlock the meanings of prejudice hang from one ring and in the Christian understanding of the problem that ring, from which all other interpretations dangle, is the innate, inevitable, yet sinful self-centeredness of the human soul. The social scientists and the psychologists shy away from the assertion that prejudice is natural, that it is indigenous to human nature, that we are "born prejudiced," perhaps in the fear that having made such a confession they must then say with the man in the street, "Prejudice is natural and nothing can be done about it. Christian doctrine, however, holds that prejudice in its pristine nucleus is natural and that something can be done about it. It makes "the hazardous assumptions regarding instincts" not solely, if certainly, on a Biblical basis but also by its long survey of the behavior of man and by theological reflections which in their mainstream have never deviated from the conviction that egocentricity, self-love, lies at the base of all interpersonal frictions.

This view is not, to be sure, a Christian exclusive. Sigmund Freud, for one non-Christian, has expressed it directly: "In the undisguised antipathies and aversion which people feel toward strangers with whom they have to do, we recognize the expression of self-love, of narcissism." Yet it is in Christian expression that this idea finds its systematic formulations. The historian Arnold Toynbee, for instance, gives this description: ". . . every living creature is striving to make itself into a centre of the Universe, and, in the act, is entering into rivalry with every other living creature. . . . Self-centredness is thus a necessity of Life, but this necessity is also a sin. Self-centredness is an intellectual error because no living creature is in truth the centre of the Universe; and it is also a moral error, because no living creature has a right to act as if he were the centre of the Universe."[19]

William Temple used a similar illustration, giving it a more definite theological application: "When we open our eyes as babies we see the world stretching out around us; we are in the middle of it. . . . I am the centre of the world I see; where the horizon is depends on where I stand. Now just the same thing is true at first of our mental and spiritual vision. . . . So each of us takes his place in the centre of his own world. But I am not the centre of the world, or the standard of reference as between good and bad; I am not, and God is. In other words, from the beginning I put myself in God's place. This is my original sin. I was doing it before I could speak, and everyone else has been doing it from early infancy."[20] Reinhold Niebuhr relates this inherent and original self-centeredness specifically to racial prejudice: "Racial prejudice, the contempt of the other group, is an inevitable concomitant of racial pride; and racial pride is an inevitable concomitant of the ethnic will to live."[21] Thus we see that self-centeredness is the essence of all sin and that prejudice is a specific expression of that sin.

The difference between prejudice in its beginnings and prejudice in its maturities may be as vast as the difference between the spermatozoon and the elephant which it produces; but whatever it may become in its various developments, in the extensions and intricacies which characterize it when it is fully grown, prejudice in germ is prideful, willful, and inevitable self-centeredness. The habitat does not produce the elephant, and the social order does not generate spermatozoic prejudice. Prejudice is protean in its effects and pristine in its origin; it is specific in origin and diffused in effect.

[19] Arnold Toynbee, *A Historian's View of Religion,* Oxford University Press, New York, 1956, pp. 4–5.

[20] William Temple, *Christianity and the Social Order,* a Pelican Series reprint, 1956, Penguin Books, Ltd., Harmondsworth, Middlesex, England, p. 52.

[21] Reinhold Niebuhr, *The Children of Light and the Children of Darkness,* Charles Scribner's Sons, New York, 1944, p. 139.

Prejudice is, therefore, "deeper and much more universal than is understood in our liberal culture."[22] It arises from the inmost center of the personality, the human will, and is at home in every human being. In the Christian view man is not at birth a *tabula rasa* upon which the natural world and society are to write all that he is to know and be; he is not a "nothingness" which will be nurtured by society into a "somethingness." Rather he comes equipped with a self which has a capacity for love and a proclivity for hatred. Whether he become an apostle of love or a disciple of hate or vacillate all his life between the two depends, in the Christian view, not solely upon the socializing forces but much more upon his acceptance or his denial of the grace of God.

The secrets of race prejudice, being internal, do not reveal themselves through sociological data, and prejudice in its aboriginal form is impervious to all sociological techniques. Whatever the beneficial results of judicial, education, and economic pressures upon the discriminative and oppressive patterns of society—a subject to which we shall soon return—such pressures have negligible effect upon prejudice per se. When we have catalogued all the sociological and educational factors, we still have left untouched the heart of the matter. Prejudice, in the Christian view, is not something which takes place on the periphery of man, as though he had acquired a stain upon the garments of personality by brushing up against the social order; it has its locus rather in the deep interior of man's being. It is not something from which he suffers as though it were a contagious disease which a corrupt society has breathed into his innocent face. It is rather a congenital disease which he brings into the world and into society, a part of his own recalcitrant, self-centered, and prideful will. Racial thinking is related to race only incidentally, we might even say accidentally. The white man is not prejudiced against the Negro because the Negro is a Negro but rather because within all men there are compulsions which, when they erupt in the white American, find in the Negro a ready, visible, and socially approved victim. If this were not so,

[22] *Ibid.*, p. 139.

we should be confronted by an otherwise baffling fact: the prejudice exhibited by minorities against minorities and against the members of their own group. We are preoccupied with the major problem—the relationship of whites to Negroes—but we must not ignore the fact that prejudice is universal. And in this fact we have further proof of the primary inwardness of prejudice.

Consequently the proper approach to the basic problem of racial prejudice is to examine not the object, the Negro, but the subject, the white man. Nothing that we can say academically about the Negro—his biological identity with the white man, his mental qualifications for full citizenship, his civic rights, his dignity as a human being—has primary bearing upon the white man's prejudice. Prejudice, it has been remarked, is not necessarily a psychosis, but it displays characteristics which resemble the behavior of the psychotic. It is absolutely rigid against all rational assaults; it flows around and by-passes the facts; it passes through argument and refutation, however sound and convincing, as though they did not exist. Pride and prejudice arise, not out of essential differences between peoples and the actual or supposed inferiority of the one to the other, not out of teaching situations which induce prejudice under parental, family, or social pressures, not out of the frictions of human proximity or the distrust which varies by the distance others are removed from us, but simply out of the will of every man to think more highly of himself than he ought to think. From the Christian point of view we do not ask what causes prejudice, as though it were an effect which must have arisen from some source outside of man; but we say of it, rather, that it is a part of the primordial nature of man. Myrdal identified the arena of the essential conflict: "The American Negro problem is a problem in the heart of the American."[23] He did not, however, correctly announce the principal antagonists. The battle, from the Christian point of view, is not between the American dream and the American deed, between the democracy we profess and the democracy we practice; rather, the principal and primeval battle within the American

[23] *Op. cit.*, p. xlvii.

79

heart—as in all hearts—is the war between the self and the not-self.

If, then, prejudice arises, not in the social setting, but in the heart of man, why are there areas of the world where there seems to be a paradisiacal innocence of racial prejudice? Why do little children in interracial settings show a complete indifference to the color of their playmates? The simple explanation is that *racial* hostility in children is not a primary instinct; but undifferentiated hostility, an aggressiveness against all and anything which thwarts and frustrates self-will, is a primary instinct. Aggressive self-assertiveness, as any parent could testify, comes with the littlest child. Even in the moment of birth he is thwarted, frustrated; his kingdom is overthrown; and, having "no language but a cry," he makes his indiscriminate protest. As we shall see, that protest, when it comes under the tutelage of society, is directed, is given shape and substance, is provided an object.

Race prejudice is learned; religious bigotry is learned; social snobbery is learned; but they can be learned only because they have an apt and eager pupil in the inherently prideful and instinctively prejudiced will of man. We do not have an inherent antipathy for certain colors or particular physical attributes; what we do have is a dominant, built-in preference for self over all that is not-self. The social setting, the teaching situation, says to the child: "We know exactly how you feel; here, then, in the Negro, in the Jew, in the latest immigrant, in the rich or in the poor, we give you an approved object for that feeling." The social setting thus provides a legitimate object for that undifferentiated prejudice with which each child is endowed. Or, if the child be fortunate and the teaching situation be wise, the social setting says to the child, "We know exactly how you feel; but nowhere in this world is there an approved object for that feeling. Therefore, your willful self-assertiveness must be conquered and transcended."

The apparent absence of racial prejudice in Brazil and Hawaii must not be cited as evidence that prejudice itself has been obliterated. Brazil has its own particular problems of prejudice, its own forms of social tension, which appear more and more to indicate a society divided along class rather than racial lines. This is apparent in the commonly known fact that in Brazil a poor white man is called a Negro and a rich Negro is called white.[24] From the polyracial character of the Hawaiian social order and its commendable tolerance of racial and national differences we can conclude only that racial and national prejudices have been superficially eliminated or somewhat controlled; we cannot conclude from these facts that there is in Hawaii a social solidarity which is in no way bisected by forces having the effect if not the face of racial prejudice. Carey McWilliams has shown how labor disputes in Hawaii have broken along racial lines: "Again in 1949 the heterogeneous elements making up the ILWU [International Longshoremen's and Warehousemen's Union] won a spectacular victory in the islands. In this viciously contested strike, the population divided sharply on racial and class lines. Indeed the demarcation was so clear-cut and precise that the union was accused of fomenting racial hatred by simply appealing to the workers on class lines. The pretense that racial prejudice does not exist in the islands was dispelled overnight."[25] "On the whole, it may be said that the several races live together in relationships which are characterized by harmony and friendliness. . . . Beneath this apparently calm surface, however, are found inequality, discrimination, prejudice, cynicism, and bitterness."[26] Indeed, "in spite of the doctrine and practice of racial equality, the race and nationality groups are not equal in terms of cultural status, social prestige, and economic power and political influence."[27]

Amalgamation in the Brazilian or Hawaiian style, when given sufficient time, will certainly solve the problem of ethnic hostility

[24] Donald Pierson, *Negroes in Brazil,* The University of Chicago Press, Chicago, 1942.

[25] *Op. cit.,* p. 193.

[26] William C. Smith, "Minority Groups in Hawaii," *The Annals of the American Academy of Political and Social Science,* September, 1942, pp. 40 and 43.

[27] Kenneth Little, *Race and Society,* UNESCO, Paris, 1952, p. 31.

by the simple removal of all lines of racial demarcation. That has happened to every people now thinking of themselves as racially pure or culturally homogeneous. But amalgamation has no effect upon prejudice as such, and in all societies new lines of distinction and discrimination appear even as the old lines fade. The hope for paralleling societies, for racial groups which occupy the same territory, the same economy, a common culture, but which maintain their racial "purity," is a delusion having little basis in the long history of man and even less support from the recent history of race relationships in America. But amalgamation as a deliberate policy would be, not the cure of prejudice, but a surrender to it. Kelly Miller saw that, from the viewpoint of the Negro, amalgamation as an avowed policy would be "self-stultification with a vengeance."[28] The basic problem is not solved so long as the Negro sees advantage in the flight from racial identity; but, as a matter of fact, miscegenation has already removed the pure Negro from the American scene. The number of Negroes in America who have no Caucasian ancestors diminishes rapidly; but prejudice does not diminish.

Therefore, viewed historically, racial prejudice, in the Christian sense, is not really a new thing but simply the latest and most virulent form of man's ancient urge for self-exaltation. Thus far, the history of antagonistic human relationships, despite the many varieties, has a single, simple, and inclusive definition: it is the story of the periodic substitution of one bias for another; it is the story, not of the correction of prejudice, but of the conversion of prejudice from one object to another; it is the story of a central and consistent motivation in the will of man, assuming at different times and in different places various cloaks and armors and assorted victims. The circles defining the "in-group" and the "out-group" have circumferences that rove and shift, now including and then excluding the same peoples; but the center of each such circle remains constant, that center being the prideful self-cen-

[28] Kelly Miller, *Race Adjustment,* The Neale Publishing Company, New York, 1910, p. 49.

teredness of the individual. Racial prejudice is merely one of these shifting and recurrent circles, a social manifestation of the individual's innate sense of personal superiority to all that lies outside the hard core of his self-centered will. Racism, as Ruth Benedict put it, is merely "a new way of separating the sheep from the goats. . . . Racism is the new Calvinism which asserts that one group has the stigmata of superiority and the other those of inferiority."[29] The Jew had his gentile; the Greek had his barbarian; the Roman had his non-Roman; the crusaders had their infidel; the fifteenth-century Roman Catholics had their heathens; the English had their Irish; the Lutherans had their Anabaptists; the Nazis had their non-Aryans; and now the white man has his Negro. Every "in-group" has an "out-group" upon which it projects all that is by its standards abhorrent and in which by contrast it sees its own glorification reflected. If we press toward the exact center of the concentric circles of inclusion and exclusion we find there the lone individual in proud and splendid isolation from the rest of mankind.

Let us see now what prejudice becomes in its extreme form, picturing for a moment what prejudice means to the soul of the utterly degenerate racist or religious bigot. Prejudice is to him what alcohol is to the alcoholic—not a problem but a solution. Without it, the extremely prejudiced person loses his sense of identity; he becomes a faceless creature. Stripped of his prejudices he becomes emotionally insecure, the prey of an indescribable sense of panic. For prejudice is his necessary narcotic. It dulls the intolerable ache of inferiority; it rationalizes his failures and disappointments; it displaces his frustrations; it projects to some external object his unbearable sense of personal guilt and shame; it focuses and gives expression to his otherwise undefined anxieties. Prejudice becomes "the very tissue of his existence"; he is the summary of his negative attitudes toward other people; remove them and he is nothing. Only by the props of prejudice does his image

[29] Ruth Benedict, *Race—Science and Politics,* Modern Age Books, New York, 1940, p. 5.

of personal identity remain erect. Only in the mirror of those as-persions which he casts against the other person can he see re-flected in contrast what he calls himself.

We have, in the words of Herman Bahr, German Social Demo-crat of the last generation, a striking and penetrating illustration both of the command which prejudice in its grotesque forms has over its subject and of the deep satisfactions which it gives him. He says, "The rich take to opium and hashish. Those who cannot afford them become anti-Semites. Anti-Semitism is the morphine of the small people. . . . Since they cannot attain the ecstasy of love they seek the ecstasy of hatred."[30] The racial or religious bigot must, in other words, rely upon his prejudices for intensity of feel-ing, for an acute awareness of being, for the meaning of his life. The fact that prejudice is a solution which does not solve, which, indeed, compounds the problem and always avenges itself upon the prejudiced is to him meaningless and inconsequential; he re-turns to his prejudices as the addict does to the needle and the al-coholic to his bottle. Why should he heed those who would save him from his prejudice when he knows that prejudice is his salva-tion!

This, however, is prejudice in its extreme deterioration, a hide-ous and repulsive picture in which unfortunately the genteel prej-udice of cultured and well-meaning people catches no glimpse of itself. We see no connection between this monstrous ugliness and our own relatively mild distaste for people of another color, an-other race; we are not aware of any connection between those who lynch the Negro or do him violence in race riots and that conven-tional prejudice which we reveal in thoughtless word and spon-taneous gesture. But the difference between the mood of the com-monly condemned extreme racist and the relatively benign, rigidly controlled, or artfully concealed prejudice of respectable people is not a difference in kind but a difference in degree. Prej-udice in the one is a full harvest of tares; in the other it is a quiet

[30] Quoted by P. W. Massing in *Rehearsal for Destruction*, Harper & Broth-ers, New York, 1949, p. 99.

but potent seed. In the one this is what prejudice has done; in the other this is what prejudice could do. Where it is merely repressed, controlled, and not removed, prejudice is a dormant malignancy which should be, but usually is not, frightening in its possibilities.

In the Christian definition, moreover, prejudice must be given an even deeper dimension. There is no sin which is not primarily or ultimately a sin against God. Prejudice in its ultimate reduction is a specific manifestation of the innate and inevitable self-centeredness of every human being, a self-centeredness which, carried to its logical and final extreme, must exclude God. Racial prejudice is an externalized and objectified form of that self-centeredness, a visible part of that invisible pride which must subdue all rivals and whose last rival is God. We can say, therefore, that prejudice, put theologically, is one of man's several neurotic and perverted expressions of his will to be God. This is an indictment of unregenerate human nature which is so utterly condemning that we find its statement primarily in the Biblical record or in the boastful confessions of those "terrible men" who in shocking words show what evil things the deep pits of the human soul can contain. Nietzsche, for example, said, "If there were a God, I could not endure not being he." This was not a clever turn of words calculated to surprise and stun its hearers and attract their attention but was for Nietzsche that honest, vulgar truth which most men would be too timid, too polite, or too crafty to confess. He committed the gross, crude *faux pas* of saying out loud what many men feel deeply, perhaps unconsciously, certainly undefined in the center of their being. He boastfully displayed that "inordinate, criminal, and suicidal pride" which reigns in all men who, in Pauline language, do not "like to acknowledge God. . . ."

In the Christian view we are not permitted the consolation of believing that prejudice, if it does harm at all, hurts only a few insignificant people who, after all, are callous and apathetic; behind the man is the man's God and it is against Him that our prejudice has sinned. We are not permitted to look outward and charge the evils of prejudice to a corrupt world. We are not allowed the balms of that fatalism which blames the blind, insensitive, uncontrollable forces of history. We can only look inward and say, "my own most grievous sin." To find the guilt anywhere outside myself, to project the blame anywhere so long as I get it outside my own soul, to confer the responsibility for the removal of prejudice upon education, the law, or some other socializing agency is merely to fortify the soul's sense of supreme innocence and superiority. As has been warned, this says nothing about the victims of prejudice, those who bear in body and soul the wounds of oppressive hatred; it says nothing about the scourges of discrimination and segregation in our society; it says nothing about strategies and tactics for the removal of such scourges; this must follow. But it does locate the habitat of prejudice; it does say that prejudice, all forms of it, is rooted in the sinful will of every man to surmount, by their extinction if necessary, all other men and at last to assault in final challenge the sovereignty of God. "I know positively," says one of Camus's characters, "that each of us has the plague within him; no one, no one on earth is free from it."[31] In the area of our concern the plague is prejudice; it is within us and no one is entirely free from it.

If, then, prejudice is such a deeply ingrained part of the essential nature of man, what shall we say about the Christian solution to the problem of prejudice? Let us remember as we turn to the answering of this question that we are here concerned not with the victims of prejudice, those who are oppressed and offended, or with what can be done for them in the milieu of social dynamics. We shall see, in fact, that education, the civilizing effects of our democratic creed, the climate of tolerance fostered by our social agencies, and the judicial restraints can maintain a better society than the exploration of the depths of human nature would indicate. Fortunately, a certain artificial and polite harmony between persons of different racial origins and cultural status does

[31] Albert Camus, *The Plague*, tr. from the French by Stuart Gilbert, Alfred A. Knopf, New York, 1948, p. 229.

not depend upon their being a universally redeemed people. We can behave better socially than we are personally and most of us do. But we are here concerned about that canker of prejudice which decays the soul of the individual. How can it be removed?

To that question Christian doctrine replies that the solution, however difficult, lies well within the range of possibility. The Christian faith declares, in the words of Viktor Frankl, that "Certainly man has instincts, but those instincts do not have him. We have nothing against instincts, nor against a man's accepting them. But we hold that such acceptance must also presuppose the possibility of rejection."[32] Man is not an immutable substance upon which heredity has set an unbreakable seal, nor is he a plastic which flows helplessly into whatever molds environment provides. He is a free moral agent, free in the radical sense of freedom, free not only to accept what is best in his heredity and to reject what is worst in his environment but also to accept or reject that which is offered to him as a spiritual being, apart from heredity or from environment.

Here, to be sure, we run the risk of that rebuke which is so frequently and often justly leveled against professional Christians: the charge that we describe the problem in extravagant terms and then dismiss it with the platitudinous suggestion that all a man has to do to solve the problem is to "accept Christ." This is a language by which Christians may or may not describe that transformation of personality which gives it a new center, some core other than self. But in the use of such highly symbolic and sectarian expressions it is well to recognize that we are in danger of losing those who need what the Christian faith has to offer. What do we mean when we say that what is offered to man by God is a new being in Christ Jesus? We say in Christian phraseology that a man can be a creature of heredity and environment or that he can be a new creation in Christ. We say that the determinant forces which play upon his life and give him his option are not two but three:

[32] Viktor E. Frankl, *The Doctor and the Soul*, Alfred A. Knopf, New York, 1955, p. xviii.

heredity, environment, and the spirit of God. We say that he becomes a new creation not first by altering the circumference of his being but by having the center of that being displaced by that which is truly central in the universe. His relationship to other people is altered, not by the social demands and not because the people have changed, but because he has been altered. We claim in our Christian description of the solution that prejudice is conquered when a man can truly say with Paul, ". . . it is no longer I who live, but Christ who lives in me."[33] But are we in these claims suggesting that we can be absolved of prejudice only by the instrumentalities of a sectarianism which can be itself a form of bigotry? Does the Christian answer to racial prejudice exclude the Jew, the Buddhist, the secularist?

Thirty-four years ago Robert E. Speer, in one of the few books which have sought "the Christian view of these questions," said, "The deepest conviction back of this book is that the Son of God, Jesus Christ, is the one solution of the race problem as of every other moral and social problem."[34] No one who knew Dr. Speer could charge him with being either arrogant, ignorant, or presumptuous in his personal life; indeed, we should want to offer his gentle spirit as evidence of the power of Christ in a human life. Even so, in the light of what has happened in the intervening years it must be conceded that insofar as the race problem is a social problem the Christ of the church is not the only solution. There are other potent remedies, allies of and available to the uses of the Christian faith. We might claim that insofar as they do the will of Christ these secular and non-Christian forces are under the lordship of Christ. But it is a lordship which they do not recognize and which they do not have to acknowledge in order to maintain their efficiency as correctives of an unjust social order.

But if the solution is to be preventative rather than merely remedial, if the problem is to be solved at its source, if the solution

[33] Galatians 2:20.
[34] Robert E. Speer, *Of One Blood,* Missionary Education Movement (Friendship Press), New York, 1924, Preface, p. v.

is to be internal and individual as well as external and social, then it is not enough to shift the passions of prejudice from one object to another, one minority to another, to exchange scapegoats, to bottle the fermentations of prejudice within the bosom of man, to limit the effects of prejudice through education and legislation. Such programs may relieve the Negro from discrimination, but they do not cure prejudice in the white man or, for that matter, in the Negro. What is essential is not some religious shibboleth but the actual invasion of the individual human life by a spirit which is able to command the center of that life. For that spirit we Christians have an adequate and completely satisfactory title; but it should not be and is not here claimed that the solution of the internal problems of prejudice is sectarian. One does not have to be a nominal Christian, to be a member of the Christian church, to "name the name of Jesus" in the sense of using certain sounds and hieroglyphics in order to have some part of the miracle of Christ in the heart. There are Jews like Martin Buber, Hindus like Gandhi, and multitudes of little people in whom self has been, not crushed and subdued, but transcended and transformed. Men do receive a spirit they cannot identify and for which they have no title; they are visited by a God whose name they do not know. When we say that Jesus Christ, the Son of God, is "the only solution," we are saying that prejudice gives way only to that spirit of God which for us was personified in the historical Jesus and which for us is the Christ. We do not presume to bind in doctrinal terms the scope and operation of that spirit; but we do say that nothing other than what we have seen and known and experienced in him will be equal to that pretender who reigns in the human heart, whose will it is to set man against man, and who has racial prejudice for one of his names.

5.

Discrimination and
the Right to Have

---

*Because men do not fortify justice,
they justify force.*
—PASCAL

Injustice against the Negro in the United
States is vast in its scope and multiple in its origins. Like the ban-
yan, it spreads over a great area and sends down many roots. The
extent of such oppression, reaching into every phase of Negro life,
is common knowledge. Excluded from public institutions, from
schools, libraries, swimming pools, golf links, parks, restaurants,
hotels; restricted in the main to menial labor, inferior housing, undesirable neighborhoods; deprived of his vote, of the legal redress
of wrongs committed against him, and of those common courtesies
which are standard etiquette between men who consider themselves equals; stereotyped by literature, by advertisements, by
humor, and by forms of entertainment which defame his race,
asperse his character, and ridicule his intellect—he is a man thoroughly, deliberately, and systematically suppressed into a secondary role in American culture. The fact that there are those

Negroes who by unusual ability and fortitude have risen to fame and the fact that there are other Negroes, particularly in the entertainment field, whom white America exhibits in pride, lauds, and pampers merely add accent to the assertion that the race as a whole has a meager and begrudged share in the blessings of a prosperous land.

Many of our references will again naturally be to the South where racial injustice is bold and extreme and where the nature and the effect of racial oppression are easily demonstrated. But from this we are not to infer that the problem is regional or that we are preoccupied with that section of the country where the problem is most acute. The writer knows, from his residence in other parts of the country and with a firsthand knowledge, that it was in Yonkers, New York, during his pastorate there, that Negroes and Jews were excluded from the inner circles of a Tuberculosis Association which had become a club for the genteel white citizens of the city; it was in Minneapolis, Minnesota, that Negro friends of his had their food salted in a Chinese restaurant and were refused the use of the clubhouse of the American Automobile Association; it was in Rochester, New York, that a brilliant, attractive Negro social worker was so harassed in his search for decent housing for his family that he finally surrendered and took his talents elsewhere; it was in Chicago that mob violence against a Negro family which had moved into a theretofore white community required a constant police patrol to insure its safety. These are incidents which could be many times multiplied to show that the problems of discrimination are nation-wide.

Where the Negro is an insignificant minority, oppressive restrictions are or have been suffered instead by other minority groups—the Indian and the Mexican in the Southwest; the Indian and the relocated Japanese in the Dakotas; the Japanese and Chinese in California; etc. But the migration of the Negro from the South to all parts of the United States suggests the possibility that what is now open and obvious in the South may find covert or flagrant repetition in all parts of the country. The concern of these words is for the Negro wherever he is; and we shall observe the patterns of discrimination wherever they thrust themselves upon us. We cannot do so without giving what might seem to be abusive attention to the problem as it appears where the great majority of Negroes are still concentrated.

The words *discrimination* and *segregation* have in our time suffered from a loose and interchangeable usage. We shall therefore make a distinction between them and give to each a specific definition. Discrimination is by definition the denial of the right to have on the basis of wholly irrelevant human considerations; it cuts a man or a people away from that which is rightfully theirs, or to which they have the right to aspire, on the basis of artificial, arbitrary, or extraneous distinctions between human beings. Because of his color, his race, his religion the victim of discrimination is withheld from that which is his natural right as a man, his civic right as a citizen, or his sacred right as a child of God. The Negro is a man but is frequently coerced solely because of his race into a life which is not befitting to the elemental dignities of his manhood; he pays local taxes but is debarred from municipal services; he defends his country in time of war but is intimidated at the polls; he has a mind but is hampered in the training of it; he has skills but no place to use them; he bears in his soul the imprint of the image of God but is oppressed as though he were not even a man. He is deprived of a fundamental human right: the right to have.

All considerations of discrimination fall, therefore, into the area of justice and injustice. That is, we are considering now not what a man should get because we are charitable toward him or because in the spirit of fairness we want to grant him favors; rather we are considering what is *his* by the rights of a primal order but from which he has been severed solely on the basis of some superficial and insignificant physical or cultural or religious characteristic. Injustice denies the right to have; justice honors the equitable application of the right to have. Some summary definitions of justice elevate it, ontologically, to the level of love.[1] This may be true in the mysteries of a high and intricate theology. However, it is better for our purposes to define justice, as we do, in the narrow Aristotelian sense as "rendering to each man his due," meaning by the term a distributive justice which dispenses to each man what is due to him as a man, a citizen, or a kinsman. "Justice," said Emil Brunner, using this limited definition, "is always concerned with mine and thine, and for that very reason, never with the person *qua* person, but with the person in view of 'something.' "[2] This is a view of the meaning of justice which not only rings true but is also immediately applicable to the problems of racial discrimination. Brunner says further, "The sphere of justice embraces all that 'belongs,' all that is a man's due, all that he has a 'right to.' "[3] (He is here using the word *belongs* in the sense of having.) Justice, then, as we shall use the word, is the relationship which ought to exist between person and person or between persons regarding a "something," a thing or condition. That "something" may be in the material domain: a piece of property, a swimming pool, a school, an eating place; or it may be in the intangible realm: the right to vote, to be employed, to be promoted on merit. But in every case distributive justice is concerned about that "something" not *in vacuo* but in reference to the rights of persons. It is concerned not that a "something" should be where it ought to be but that people should have what they ought to have.

That justice is never cold and impersonal is attested by the fact that injustice always establishes a personal relationship—a relationship of hostility between the depriver and the deprived—and inflicts upon the deprived either injury to his physical welfare or offense to his spirit. We can speak of justice on the human plane only in terms of at least two persons and at least one thing

[1] Paul Tillich, *Love, Power, and Justice,* Oxford University Press, New York, 1954, p. 13.
[2] Emil Brunner, *Justice and the Social Order,* Harper & Brothers, New York, 1945, p. 17.
[3] *Ibid.,* p. 18.

or condition. However much we may curse the perversity of in-animate objects, we know that things are never unjust. We may speak of a law as being unjust but the law had its formulators and has its executors and it is they who, wittingly or not, are just or unjust. We may speak of customs and conventions as unjust, but these are merely labels for the lengthened and thoughtless habits of the people. If a fire should destroy the public library in that little Southern town in which I grew up, the people would suffer, not an injustice, but a misfortune. But the Negro, who is a member of the public and a citizen of that town, suffers an in-justice when, because of his race, he is deprived of the free use of that library. And the injustice is inflicted, not by an impersonal system or by an impartial accident, but by the people—the ad-ministrator, the board, and the white citizenry. If a hurricane should destroy all the public schools in that town and all resources for their restoration, that would be a calamity; but to deprive some of the children on account of their race of the right to use the facilities of all the schools is an injustice; and the blame falls not upon fortune but upon people. Injustice is that human rela-tionship in which people deprive other people of the right to have on the basis of irrelevant considerations; justice is the equitable application of the right to have. Racial injustice deprives a man of the right to have on the basis of his race; racial justice honors and enforces his right to have irrespective of his race.

The Judeo-Christian faith has been concerned not merely about the regeneration and the saving of the individual soul, not merely about a pervasive, universal love which might make considera-tions of justice unnecessary. It has, on the contrary, been vitally concerned about distributive justice, "the rendering to each man his due." It has been the loudest and the longest protest against those injustices by which men rob men of their rights; it has been the strongest and the most consistent champion of the rights of men in material as well as spiritual domains. It has boldly de-nounced even mercy, charity, and love where these have not satis-fied the elemental claims of justice. It has wisely known that sweet pleadings, appeals to fair play, and moral suasions of all sorts cannot alone abolish social injustices. It has confidently professed a righteous God who demands righteousness of his children; and it has professed that man is made in the image of God and that, in Calvin's words, "we must hold him sacred in such a way that he cannot be injured without the image of God being injured at the same time." But we have seen that the Christian church in its relationships to the Negro has not kept, proclaimed, and practiced its own faith. What, then, can and should the church do to implement its ethic and to help abolish racial injustice?

To answer that question we must for a time investigate the varied roots of racial discrimination. We know, to note one of its roots, that racial injustice, the denial of the right to have on the basis of race, is the product of racial prejudice, an overt expression of racial pride. The church, therefore, has the major, incessant, and preventative task of changing the hearts of men through the power of the Gospel and the grace of God, reorienting their lives around God instead of themselves. It must profess, teach, and practice that inclusive Christian love which penetrates and transcends the barriers of race. It must proclaim that whole truth which it has received in Christ Jesus, the truth that every man is a fallen but beloved and redeemable child of God, "a lost coin with the King's inscription upon it," and that all have a created oneness in God, a tragic oneness in sin, and a restored oneness in Christ. In a word, the church must bear witness to its Lord, to His sovereignty in the human soul, and to that oneness which all men have in Him.

But if this is all, it is not enough. It may suffice for the removal of individual cases of personal prejudice; it is not sufficient for the removal of racial injustice. While we are busy grubbing out the emotional, the spiritual, roots of discrimination, the other roots send themselves deeper, anchoring the vile plants of social injustice in a thicker and equally nourishing soil. And those other roots by which racial discrimination is sustained and nurtured cannot be cut by reason and conscience. Here we can take the counsel of Reinhold Niebuhr to the effect that ". . . a too consistent optimism in regard to man's ability and inclination to grant justice to his fellows obscures the perils of chaos which perennially confront every society, including a free society."[4] Or we can draw our conclusion from the plain, historical fact that there has been no significant instance in which the white society motivated by love and mercy has voluntarily relinquished an area of domination over the Negro. On the contrary, every major social advancement made by the Negro has resulted from some kind of legal or social coercion. It would be folly to assume that the barriers which still stand between the Negro and his full manhood will topple before a trumpet of justice which is not accompanied by any kind of force. Whether Booker T. Washington's opinion was politically naïve or a wise strategy fitted to his difficult time, we know now that one of his programs failed him—his hope that "the opportunity to freely exercise such political rights will not come in any large degree through outside or artificial forcing, but will be accorded to the Negro by the Southern white people themselves, and that they will protect him in the exercise of those rights."[5] If it was a plea, it fell upon deaf ears; if a strategy, it failed. But there is more than one weapon in the arsenal of the Christian faith; and, though love may be "the greatest of these," it is not alone.

To see what else the church and Christian people must do we must examine some of the other sources from which racial discrimination draws its virility. In some cases, certainly, racial discrimination is nothing more than a part of the general struggle for economic and political power with no reference to race except for the fact that the Negro is an easy and available victim. When man enslaves, he puts into bondage those who are most easily enslaved; when he exploits, he uses those who are most easily ex-

[4] Reinhold Niebuhr, *The Children of Light and the Children of Darkness*, Charles Scribner's Sons, New York, 1944, Foreword, p. xi.
[5] Booker T. Washington, *Up From Slavery*, The Sun Dial Press, Garden City, N.Y., 1937, p. 234.

ploited. In our day the Negro is an available and socially approved victim and discrimination against him is therefore in many instances not a part of the racial conflict but more properly a part of the class struggle. Indeed, it has been suggested by some that the official perpetuation of the doctrine of racial inferiority and superiority in the South is merely a bribe by which the poor whites themselves are kept contented as an exploited class. Whether that is true or not, it is certain that doctrines of racial inferiority and superiority are some times a pretense for exploitation. We cannot with Oliver C. Cox make an exhaustive gospel out of the economic explanation of racial oppression. We have said, in fact, that to describe prejudice in economic terms is to describe duplicity rather than prejudice. But to ignore the contribution which exploitation makes to racial discrimination is to make a superficial study of the nature of racial injustice.

Years ago Booker T. Washington, in an abortive appeal to the white man's enlightened self-interest, said that the white man cannot keep the Negro in the ditch without staying there with him. Over the long reaches of history that may be true. But this is history seen from the long view. The ordinary man, considering what is good and profitable, is myopic. He is concerned about what happens to him immediately: who gets the available job; who upgraded in the firm and who remains in the menial capacity; who engineers the trains, pilots the planes, holds the political offices, monopolizes the professions, clips the coupons. When the racial system gives the white man preference and advantage simply by virtue of his color, it is to be expected that he will find ways and means of continuing that system. Consequently, the Southerner, aided by Northern sympathizers, fought successfully the establishing of a Permanent Fair Employment Practices Commission on a national level, excluded the Negro from artisan labor unions, arbitrarily limited the educational opportunities of Negroes who might compete with white people for professional and political offices; and, to justify himself, preserved from a slave economy the fiction that Negroes are natively inferior and are incapable of holding such positions and performing such services.

Secondly, we must remember that patterns of racial discrimination in the United States are not necessarily and always deliberately and intentionally discriminatory. Rather, they can be the unconscious behavior of the dominant and subservient groups. Although the human factor is implicit in most patterns of discrimination, in this case it is as though the Negro were the victim of some vast, impersonal conspiracy and as though the conduct of the white man were ordered by forces over which he has no control. We shall see in a moment that there actually are ironic twists of history which apart from all human involvements play havoc with human relations and require for their untangling a concerted, organized, and forceful social effort. But here we are concerned with those patterns of discrimination which *seem* impersonal in motivation, which are of such long duration, which are so deep in the habits of "white ways," which are so fortified by and congealed in customs and laws, as to be taken for granted by most whites and by many Negroes. Not only are such systems of oppression thoughtlessly accepted and unconsciously observed but they also have an obstinate resistance, an imperviousness, to any suggestion that they are unjust.

When, for example, a white or Negro child first becomes conscious of the social system into which he has been born, however short-lived the system may be, he will, as a rule, conclude that the world as he has found it is as it should be. To him this is the way things are and whatever is, is right. In such a situation there will be some Negroes who have a protesting and rebelling spirit; there will be some whites who sense that what is, is wrong; but the masses of both races will thoughtlessly accept the *status quo* as being a divine or fated order which they are born, not to contest, but to observe. The ordinary white person in the South opens his eyes on a world in which taxis, taverns, cemeteries, and toilets, schools, drinking fountains, waiting rooms, and hotels are segregated not merely by custom but even more by law. Taught to

98

revere custom and honor the law he begins to do mechanically, by reflex, what custom and the law have provided as sanctioned patterns of conduct. The Negro in the South wakes to a world in which the law describes him in unmistakable terms of inferiority, in which custom dictates the rules of his subserviency, and in which in many instances his own parents, to protect him from the dominant white group, hammer him into a conforming spirit. Through the early formative years these pressures develop in many Negroes and in most whites a placid, thoughtless acceptance of the racial codes to which they have been born. In the North whites and Negroes by the age of discernment have often been habituated to patterns of discrimination which include exclusive restaurants and hotels, restrictive covenants, Negro ghettos, gerrymandered school districts, subordinate labor roles. This is the world as they find it; and lassitude, indifference, complacency, ignorance, or fatalism keeps them either reluctant to challenge this familiar scene or cowed by the benighted assumption that this is the way things have always been and will always be. It is as though a whole people had from their earliest memory and history suffered from malaria. They are all sick; but, since their disease is universal and ancient, they mistake disease for health. To such a people sickness is normal; and to many Americans, Negroes and whites, the abnormalities of racial discrimination appear entirely normal. So it is that the white man often injures the Negro without any malicious desire to do so, and the Negro is wounded without any consciousness of pain.

The webs of discrimination, moreover, are exceedingly intricate, catching in their delicate but tough strands even those who are resolved to have no part in the discriminatory systems which oppress the Negro. An enlightened white businessman, for instance, may join a civic club, after determining that this particular club does not disqualify applicants on the basis of race. Shortly, he discovers that the local club which he has joined does honor the inclusive principle of its international body but has consistently refused membership to Negro candidates. His protest is met with the news that the hotel in which the club meets refuses to serve luncheons to Negroes and that there is not in his town any hotel or restaurant which will serve meals to Negroes. The manager of the hotel says that exclusion of Negroes is the owner's policy and that he is simply obeying orders. The owner of the hotel claims that he has to make a living and that his customers would not tolerate a Negro patron in the dining room. The customers come and go and cannot be polled. By this time our enlightened businessman—if he has pursued the matter this far—has found the fellowship of the club enjoyable and profitable. He therefore remains in a role which he had formerly abhorred, telling himself that he will stay in and do what good he can.

Or, for another example, a Southerner may want to show to Negroes those elemental courtesies which he shows to white people, but the law prohibits some of the courtesies he would gladly give; shall he defy the law? Furthermore, acts of courtesy which imply the social equality of Negroes would be in some cases an affront to his white neighbors, would jeopardize his acceptance by his own people, would subject him to economic retaliations by an incensed white community; shall he alienate many people in order to show respect for a few? In such a setting the racial complex is so extensive, so all-embracing, that no white person can be innocent of discrimination against the Negro. No white person can escape or refund the benefits which through racial discrimination accrue to all white people. However much he may decry the injustices of the system and however sincerely he may want to escape its contagions, he remains, however reluctantly, a beneficiary of the Negro's loss, a participant in a social order which he may denounce but from which he cannot entirely escape. He is caught up, for all the purity of his passion for the Negro's welfare, in the meshes of a system which produces benefits for him at the expense of the Negro. He shares inevitably, despite his protest and his repentance, in a system of human relationships which, apart from anything he may do or think, grinds out credits to him and debits to his Negro neighbor. He has not deliberately done and perhaps would not willfully do anything which turns the Negro into a means to an end, which deprives the Negro of what is rightfully his, or which degrades the Negro to some subhuman level of life; but he is immersed, nevertheless, in a way of life, in laws and folkways, which make it impossible for him to escape under his own power or by any idealism or purest conduct that <u>racial guilt in which the white man's culture involves all who are white.</u>

(3) In the third place, in examining the varied roots of racial discrimination we discover that the modes of social order are at times as much affected by blind forces as they are by human thought and effort. Alfred North Whitehead calls these blind forces "senseless agencies" and says that they and "formulated aspirations cooperate in the work of driving mankind from its old anchorage."[6] Among the "senseless agencies" he lists Steam and the Barbarians and among the "formulated aspirations" he puts Democracy and Christianity. If these are correctly stated as the two forces which drive civilizations forward, then it is also true that there are two which retard human progress: senseless agencies and formulated human resistance. The senseless agencies do not care whether man advance or retreat; their office, like that of the Fates of mythology, is "to spin the thread of human destiny . . . and . . . cut it off when they pleased."[7] This does not mean that man is therefore helpless and swept along by forces over which he has no control; but it does mean that the problems of social injustice are deeper than we think and cannot be solved by a moralizing which holds up lofty ideals and begs men to do what they ought to do.

From Charles and Mary Beard in *The Rise of American Civilization* we can draw together two illustrations of the effect of senseless agencies upon social justice: one which revived slavery and the other which smothered it to death. First, the invention

[6] Alfred North Whitehead, *Adventures of Ideas,* The Macmillan Company, New York, 1933, p. 7.

[7] Charles Mills Gayley, *Classic Myths,* Ginn and Company, Boston, 1949, p. 38.

and the patenting of the cotton gin by Eli Whitney in 1794 is a precise and frequently cited illustration of the effect of an amoral factor upon the morals of a people. Prior to this time slavery, by economic necessity, had begun to dwindle; sentiments favoring abolition were running strong in the South, even more so than in the North. But this single invention reversed that trend and gave life and vigor to the slave system for an additional seventy years. The Beards wrote, "Stirred by the volcanic energies of capitalism, slavery of the traditional type underwent a drastic change. Even in the older sections where cotton culture did not flourish and where the law of diminishing returns had threatened the ultimate extinction of chattel servitude, the institution was now given a new lease on life."[8] But by 1860 "the sweep of economic forces" had pushed the industrial North to a revenue far beyond that produced by the "rice, sugar, cotton, and tobacco of the South . . . —a fact more ominous than Garrison's abolition."[9] Thus the senseless and seemingly irreversible forces of industry and economy had in one time given the breath of life to slavery and in another time snatched it away. Preachments could have been directed against the acquisitive instincts of slaveowners or against the greed of Northern merchants and industrialists; indeed, they were. But to moralize about the presence of the cotton gin or to appeal to that insensitive industrial revolution which was sweeping the North into prosperity and the South into despair was to tilt at windmills.

The blind forces which operate in any given time are best identified by hindsight, and it requires rare prophetic vision to see the trends of any given time while they are happening. But we can hazard the guess that the vigorous and increasing industrial upheaval in the South will in the end be as much responsible for public-school desegregation as is the formulated aspiration of the 1954 Supreme Court decision. The Ford, someone

[8] Charles A. Beard and Mary R. Beard, *The Rise of American Civilization*, The Macmillan Company, New York, 1930, Vol. One, p. 655.
[9] *Ibid.*, p. 635.

has said, did more to elevate the status of the Negro than all the churches; racial etiquette is difficult to enforce on the highways. Again, it is possible that rural electrification, bringing the world into the homes of Negroes and poor whites through radio, telephone, and television, will loosen the tight taboos of discrimination which have existed between the races; it is possible that the Second World War, despite the world-wide tragedies which followed in its wake, has had enormous beneficial by-products for the American Negro; it is possible that the recent rise and success of nationalism among colored peoples in China, India, Pakistan, Ghana, the East Indies, and elsewhere will restore among Negroes respect for color; it is possible that political expediency will succeed where statesmanship has failed.

On the other hand there are blind forces, as well as deliberate human resistance, which are working to preserve the American pattern of racial injustice. Whatever else may be said here, the important fact is that patterns of social injustice, when they have been deeply engraved in a culture over a long period of time *become* senseless agencies. Racial customs, even when they are cut off from their original sources, have a self-contained momentum. They are like freely moving bodies in space: once they are set in motion they continue indefinitely until they meet a friction which exhausts their momentum or are opposed by some equal and counteracting force. The first cause is forgotten or recedes so far into the dim past that the system gathers to itself the aura of antiquity, of rightness, and even of divine sanction, as is true of the caste system in India. The systems lose through time the personal qualities, good and bad, of those through whom they were originated and they advance in the culture on their own and largely divorced from all considerations of conscience. They become the mind of the crowd, which is something more and different from the accumulated minds of the individuals. This applies not only to the mild forms of racial discrimination to which we have referred but also to the whole oppressive system. Like soil and climate, it affects men emotionally but is not itself emotional

103

or subject to emotional appeals. The social system becomes as amoral, insensitive, and nonrational about human welfare as was the coming of the atomic bomb. Being indifferent to human values it yet provides the ground for ignorant and prejudiced judgments. It crowds the Negro into shack and ghetto and rebukes him for being unclean; it deprives him of the instruments of elemental hygiene and counts his vulnerability to tuberculosis as an evidence of his inferiority; it hinders his access to the polls and offers the scarcity of registered Negro voters as evidence of political indifference; it builds in the soul of the suppressed Negro intolerable pressures of bitterness and rebellion and indicts him as exceptionally criminal; it obstructs the training of his mind and offers tests and surveys to prove that he is not the intellectual equal of the white man; it prohibits Negro children from the use of municipal parks, playgrounds, swimming pools, libraries, and tennis courts and complains that Negro children are always getting into trouble; it holds the Negro to menial jobs, prevents his being upgraded, pays him unequal wages for equal work and condemns him as lazy, listless, and lacking in ambition. Thus the social system itself becomes the soil and climate in which racial prejudice has wild and luxurious growth and drops at the end of each season a rich yield of seeds for the next crop of racial discrimination.

It is well to include among the senseless agencies governing racial discrimination for good and ill the continuing migration of the Negro into the industrial North. So long as we have an expanding economy and industry absorbing the increasing number of Negroes in the large Northern cities and industrial centers, the migration of the Negro and his congestion in these principal industrial areas may produce nothing more than minor conflicts between the several racial entities. But, given a depression and large-scale unemployment, the competition for available jobs may explode in patterns of racial strife. We have already had serious warnings of this possibility in the conflicts over housing in Northern cities and have noticed how the geographic center of racial violence has moved northward with the flow of the Negro population. If this should happen, as it is likely to, we shall have another instance of the effect of amoral forces upon the morals of a people—in this case, the effect of a senseless and undirected shifting of populations into an area in which they can no longer be absorbed by a faltering economy.

We see, then, that racial discrimination not only is a wound left by human pride but also is born of greed, of man's indifference to man, and of those dumb and heartless forces which in human history may promote or obstruct man's quest for social justice. Seeing this, we need to see also how futile it is to deal exclusively with the internal man or to treat him at all unless at the same time all possible pressures are brought to bear upon those systems in which the man is to some extent a prisoner. To wait upon the coming of universal good will, the erasure of all prejudice from the human soul, to depend solely upon the conversion of men one by one to the ways of kindness and good will is to require of the Negro that he stretch his long patience still further and be needlessly heroic and is to require of the intelligent white man that he be naïve. A social problem as deep and as damaging to personality as is this one demands that we make a simultaneous assault not only upon every citadel of pride in the human heart but also upon every senseless pattern which hobbles the body and stunts the soul of man.

For many of us, exempt as we are from the stigmas of race and free from the harassments of an oppressive social order, the questions of immediacy and gradualism, of coercion and persuasion, may seem academic. But they are not so for the Negro. Experience has for him been a dear teacher. For 246 years he languished in slavery waiting for the heart of Pharaoh to be moved; but freedom did not come until Moses went down and *told* old Pharaoh to let his people go. For many years, in response to a persuasive orator and beloved leader, the Negro let down his buckets where he was, but they always brought up a brackish water; and the water was not sweetened until he began to draw from a different and a truly "mighty stream." For decades he waited at the white man's back door, hat in hand; but he has learned that for him there is much more to be gained by standing at the front door holding, not a hat, but a subpoena. So thoroughly is the leadership of the Negro race and most of its followers converted to this new strategy that they will not be pursuaded to wait with their long hopes until there are enough men of good will to make those hopes a reality. They have measured the results of decades of waiting against the results of brief years of acting; and they no longer have a choice.

And, in a sense, neither does the white man. His time, too, has run out; the time in which he could have moved toward the plight of the Negro voluntarily, nobly, graciously, in Christian love and with credit to himself has elapsed. His options now are strictly limited: he can yield slowly and grudgingly before the advances of the Negro, delaying and harassing the progress of the Negro every step of the way, fighting a bitter rear-guard action in a lost cause; or he can co-operate with the inevitable wholeheartedly, making fully available to the Negro the instruments of racial justice and applying those instruments himself, not delaying but hastening the day when the Negro, too, shall have what is rightfully his. There will always be opportunity for individual acts of Christian good will, for something more than discrimination is involved, as we shall see, in the racial tension in America. But in reference to the Negro's right to have what is his natural, God-given, or democratic due, Christian people are henceforth divided into two camps: those who resentfully retreat before the claims of the Negro or deliberately resist those claims and those who actively participate in the Negro's struggle for racial justice.

We have thought of justice as the equitable application of the right to have, and have said that racial justice honors and enforces the right to have irrespective of race. Therefore, when we speak of racial justice, two things are presupposed: a voice for its expression and an arm for its enforcement. The voice of justice is not merely a calm, dispassionate balancing of men on the basis of rights and merits; it is not the voice of a blinded goddess holding impartial scales, measuring right and wrong, but the voice of an Amos, agitated, concerned, involved in all injuries unjustly suffered by mankind. The voice of justice is the voice of protest, dissent, condemnation. It is the prophetic voice; it uncovers and reveals the corruptions of injustice; it irritates, embarrasses, and denounces the unjust; it lays the ugliness of what is over against the beauty of what should and can be. It is the scourge of personal smugness and social complacency, the mallet and chisel for hardened hearts and caked minds, the catalyst which brings the social change to its appointed moment. The voice of justice is a harsh voice, jarring even insensitive nerves. It may be backed as it was in Jesus by immense deposits of love for the accused; but it is not softened and does not hesitate on that account.

The voice of justice is, of course, only one of the several voices of the church; but it is this prophetic voice which has been largely silenced as the white church has faced the problems of race. The church has sweetly exhorted men to do justly and love mercy but it has not thrown the revealing light of a holy God upon injustice and cruelty in the relationships of the white man to the Negro. It has helped, indeed, to conceal the enormity and the depth of the crime of racial discrimination. But the church must be prophetic; it must accuse and stand under its own accusation; it must judge and be so judged; it must uncover the corruptions of racial oppression even though in so doing its own sores are exposed. It must be censorious, however much it is humiliated by its own censure. Criticism of the social order, whatever that order, is a vital and commissioned part of the role of the church. Criticism maintains the tension between what is and what should be; in the area of race it is the irritant which prevents the congealing of ideological patterns and social customs and disturbs those which have already congealed. A criticism which tells us the hard truth about the plight of the Negro and our continuing contribution to his burden and his sorrow, whatever its source, should be greeted not as an enemy but as a friend.

Those who cry, "Leave us alone and we'll take care of it ourselves," are the very ones who must not be left alone. To those who say, "Agitators and critics only stir up trouble and make things worse and never do any good," we have to answer that historically it has not been so. Jim Crowism became a fixed folkway at a time when the church was silent and withdrawn. And Jim Crowism began to wane when justice once more found its voice, not through the church, but through those social agencies which had taken seriously the claims of American democracy. And the outsider, the alien critic, the Jonah in Nineveh and the Amos in Israel, has a role of special importance. It is through him that a people learn that their sins are visible in distant places. Criticism from the North has had, despite vehement protests from the criticized, a beneficial effect upon race relations in the South, and criticism from abroad has intensified the nation's desire to put its house in order. But the alien critic has his own special spiritual jeopardy; the temptation to self-righteousness, to hypocrisy, to be an eagle in seeing his neighbor's wrongs and a beetle in seeing his own, is always strong upon him. The Northerner in condemning racial practices in the South must remember that the spirit of the Negro can be wounded far deeper where justice is expected than it can be where injustice is taken for granted, and he must remember that it is no easy task to remove a beam from his brother's eye if he has even so little as a mote in his own. Justice must speak but human justice is always partial and must stand under its own judgments.

Justice, we have said, requires a voice for its expression; it must also have an arm for its enforcement. William Sumner, in his *Folkways,* made the extravagant claim that "Nothing but might makes right."[10] But the fact is that might never makes right. Power, in human hands, can manipulate and govern but it

[10] William Graham Sumner, *Folkways,* Ginn and Company, Boston, 1906, p. 65.

cannot generate; it determines, in the political realm, not what is right, but simply what is to be. Might can be a benevolent dictator, the champion of justice; or it can be a monstrous tyrant, the foe of justice. It was might that kept the Negro in bondage and it was might that finally set him free; but might did not determine whether slavery was right or wrong. Might can put a Negro on a bus or take him off—it has done both; but whether or not he belongs there is determined not by might but by justice. Consequently the history of human progress has been in part the story of the struggle of justice to have might as its ally; without its aid, justice has had no arm for its enforcement. It is justice, a justice which is of the essence of the righteousness of God, that determines what are men's rights; but it is might, a power which has become an instrument of the righteousness of God, that alone enforces those rights. A social justice which is not fortified, whatever justice may be in the individual life, becomes nothing more than a poetic, quixotic dreamer, forever wandering dark streets at the mercy of any villain.

Much has been made, and properly so, of the fact that the Montgomery experiment, so successfully led by Martin Luther King and his associates, was nonviolent; but little has been made of the fact that the Montgomery experiment was also coercive. Behind the Negro's claim for justice on a nondiscriminatory public utility was the overpowering fact that the bus company was primarily dependent for its income upon the Negro commuter. The nonviolent boycott of the bus company by the Negro was realistic on two counts: it was nonviolent where violence would have been not only unchristian but also suicidal for the Negro, and it was a boycott which, so to speak, had teeth in it. Justice, the right of the Negro to ride buses without discrimination, had been joined by might, an economic pressure sufficient to cause the capitulation of the bus company and the breaking of a taboo.

It is instructive to place over against the nonviolent boycott of the buses in Montgomery, Alabama, an even more striking phenomenon in Southern life. Koinonia Farm near Americus, Georgia, is committed under the leadership of Dr. Clarence Jordan to a program of interracial life and Christian pacifism which goes far beyond that of the Negroes in Montgomery. But the social justice sought by Koinonia Farm has nowhere an arm for its enforcement and has been several times on the brink of extinction. There, justice has not been able to summon might to its side. This is certainly not to decry Christian pacifism, which has its justification beyond the social scene; it is merely to point out that passive resistance in its naked aloneness seldom effects a radical change in the social order. But where nonviolent, passive resistance is supported directly or indirectly by coercive pressures, as it was under Gandhi, its effect upon societal patterns can be radical and immediate. We can expect that the Montgomery experiment will be many times successfully repeated. But its repetition in other areas must always be nonviolent—else might is crushed by superior might—and must always apply social pressures, or the threat of social pressures, which are realistically coercive. To boycott a restricted swimming pool or a segregated church, to picket a "whites only" library, to march on a state capitol in the Deep South would be to make nonviolent coercion ridiculous.

This means that there are vast areas of racial discrimination which cannot be remedied by persuasion, by education, or by the coercive action of Negroes alone. But the problem is not theirs alone; it belongs to the nation, to the whole people, and therefore to every form of government from the Supreme Court down to the least municipality. In our political tradition governments are formed, among other purposes, to "establish justice"; that is, they are formed for the express purpose of giving justice an arm for its enforcement. Justice is fortified, to paraphrase Pascal, so that men may not have to justify force. Justice is empowered by government so that the people may make a direct appeal to justice without resorting to violence. The people are given a third option wherever justice is established by government: they do not have to wait indefinitely until the social climate is changed by the changing of the hearts of men; nor are they limited to tedious, slow, and dangerous group pressures; they can appeal directly to the might which enforces justice. For the Negro, the long way home to social justice is by way of education, religious persuasion, an appeal to the spirit of democracy, and the slow perfection and application of his own native powers; and the shortcut is through congress and court, legislation and injunction.

Alfred North Whitehead said that "The recourse to force, however unavoidable, is a disclosure of the failure of civilization, either in the general society or in a remnant of individuals."[11] Laws, as we might put it, are conclusive evidence of the sinfulness of man—either the sinfulness of those who impose unjust laws or the sinfulness of those upon whom just laws are imposed. If we may adapt a phrase from Tillich, since the law cannot be wholly internalized in the conscience of imperfect man, conscience must be externalized in law.[12] This is one of the many reasons why a prejudiced and discriminatory people resent those laws which regulate the relationships between the races. They believe themselves to be a righteous, just, good people who will "do the right thing" for the Negro if they are left alone and given a chance. Legislation in the field of race insults their fair image of self by implying that they cannot be trusted to "do the right thing." But legislation is required, the recourse to force is necessary, justice has to be fortified, because man has proved that he cannot be trusted to do justly. It is regrettable that the elemental rights of human beings have to be protected by law; it is regrettable that the failure of our civilization, our failure, has to be announced to the world through such laws; it is regrettable that we are a sinful people; but we are and therefore the law which we will not obey from within must be established from without.

It will still be said, "You cannot legislate morals"; to this saying the state should answer, "We are not trying to legislate

[11] *Op. cit.*, p. 105.
[12] *Op. cit.*, p. 81.

your morals; but we can restrain your immoralities." Laws are passed not to make bad people good, but to make innocent people safe. Racial legislation is enacted and racial decrees are ordered, not to make the white man righteous but to make the Negro a full citizen, to give him what as a man and a citizen he has the right to have. No law, not even the law of God, will compel us to love the Negro; but the proper law, properly enforced, will reduce the effects of hatred, contempt, and greed upon the life of the Negro. Racial justice says to the white man, "You can have your smirking pride, your notions of superiority, your haughty airs—for these you are accountable at a higher level than justice. But their overt expression in deeds which rob your fellow man of the rights which are as sacred to him as to you, you may not have. For these you are accountable to me." Enforced justice puts the visible sin of man under judgment and restraint; it is the compromise which love makes with a sinful world.

"But," it will be said, "stateways cannot change folkways." If William Sumner, who made this saying a choice cliché with all who resist the changing of social patterns, had lived a few years longer perhaps he would have known the embarrassments of such a pronouncement. Within one country after another in our lifetime stateways have changed folkways for good and for ill. To take only one superb example, Turkey, under the dynamic leadership of Kemal Atatürk, was brought by decree out of the ancient into the modern world in one generation. By governmental fiat the centuries-old customs of a people, even in language, were overthrown and new ways imposed. This will stand where many more are available as certain evidence that the mores of a people can be altered by legislation or by decree. Indeed, in no part of the United States has there been so much change in the superficial relationships of peoples as there has been in the South in the past decade. The deep streams of traditions and conventions have been only slightly stirred, but many of the shallow customs of race relations have loosened. And this has happened through the pressure of legislative and judicial decision and despite the fact that there has been in the more recent years a tightening rather than a relaxing of racist doctrines. "The common notion that integration 'won't work' in the South is directly contradicted by the finding that some 1,100 instances of desegregation had taken place in the two year span."[13] (In the school systems of the South from 1954 to 1956.)

The experience of my own adopted state in the desegregation of the public schools is significant. West Virginia is a border state which industrially and economically is oriented toward the North but which faces south in many of its sympathies. When the Supreme Court declared the segregation of the races in the public schools unconstitutional, the State Superintendent of Free Schools, Dr. W. W. Trent, after conferring with the governor and the attorney general, instructed the county superintendents to "begin immediately to reorganize and readjust their schools to comply with the Supreme Court decision." The reaction of the people of the state was, of course, varied. The files of the State Superintendent, which he has kindly permitted the writer to examine, contain a number of letters, evidently from all walks of life, bitterly denouncing the action of the Supreme Court and the pronouncement by the State Superintendent. The files of county superintendents undoubtedly contain many similar letters. But the pleading, defiant, bitter tone of such letters in no way softened the resolution of state officials to comply fully and speedily with the decision of the Supreme Court. Resistance against the Supreme Court decision and against the action of state officials was met firmly and with dispatch by Judge Ben Moore, Federal District Judge for the Southern District of West Virginia. County officials, in the main, avoided any word or act which would indicate vacillation. As a result the desegregation of the

[13] Public Affairs Pamphlet No. 244, December, 1956, Public Affairs Committee, Inc.

public schools in West Virginia, even in districts having the largest Negro population, proceeded quickly and without serious incident.

In many situations, as was true in this one, there are many people who desire to comply with the requirements of justice. But they do not want to be the first to break with discriminatory patterns which seem to have universal approval. Laws which enforce justice and officials who firmly execute those laws bring these hesitant supporters of justice into the open. There were well-meaning, intelligent people in southern West Virginia who expected the desegregation of the public schools to initiate a reign of terror. This was an unwarranted pessimism; but an outcome exactly opposite to that gloomy expectation was due to the fact that in most of the people there were enormous deposits of justice which the cool, firm action of state, federal, and public-school officials uncovered. It is enlightening to place the West Virginia experience over against the contrasting situation in Little Rock, Arkansas, in the early fall of 1957, a situation in which the chief executive of the state by default encouraged violent resistance to federal law. West Virginia by its success and Arkansas by its failure demonstrate the fact that, given a just law and officials who are not vacillating in the enforcement of that law, folkways do surrender to stateways.

It will be said that legislation can never precede but must always follow the will of the people, that social reform can never move beyond public opinion, that "legislation, to be strong, must be consistent with the mores."[14] But such a political and social philosophy is not in agreement with the facts. The 1954 Supreme Court decision came at a time when less than half of the people of the United States approved public-school desegregation and when far more than half were still convinced that the "separate but equal" doctrine was fair and just. But there is as yet no reason to doubt either the rightness or the strength of that decision. In areas of the South where desegregation of the schools has been

[14] Sumner, *op. cit.*, p. 55.

accomplished it has been achieved despite the fact that only 31 per cent of the white population approved.[15] To be sure, legislation which is too far in advance of the people loses itself. If it precede public opinion, as in some cases it does and as in crucial cases it must, it must continually look back over its shoulder to see whether the people are following and whether it is still within the people's view. And the educating influences within the community—schools, churches, newspapers, and all the other socializing and civilizing agencies—have the responsibility of helping to bring public opinion abreast of those governmental decisions which are beyond the public will and approval but which have as their purpose the establishing of justice. In all questions of justice, in all questions involving the right of the people to have, the procedure must be to elevate the people to the level of the law rather than to lower the law to the level of the people. It is better to have laws which exceed the generosities of the people than it is to legalize by omission injustices which violate the rights and the dignities of men.

Here, then, the role of the Christian church should be obvious. In the Biblical view, specifically in the Pauline view, church and state are held to be, not incompatible, but complementary instruments of the will of God for man. Either may profane that ordination, come under the judgment and the wrath of God, and require for its redemption the grace of God. Both are continuously tempted to love power, to deny justice, and to employ violence and fraud; therefore each must defend the people against the vices of the other. Moreover, the record is that when church and state become identical—by merger or by the control of one by the other—or where they collaborate in mischief, the most abusive and stubborn forms of injustice come into force. But where each is true to its ordination as an instrument of the will of God and each serves as a check upon the other, they are not in opposi-

[15] For statistics, see *Scientific American,* December, 1956, survey by Herbert H. Hyman and Paul B. Sheatsley, for National Opinion Research Center, a comparison of attitudes 1942–1956.

tion to each other but interdependent. They represent as they confront each other the paralleling tablets of the law of God; they are the long and the short instruments of the will of God for the correction and guidance of the ways of man. The state has the short and immediate task of opposing and restraining the evil of man in any given situation; the church has the long and time-less task of seeking to bring men into the dominion of Christ and the Christian is a member of both. The state has, as Richard Niebuhr put it, the "interim function"[16] of restraining that which is evil; the church has the perennial function of proclaiming that which is good. In the performance of their separate but intertwined duties the state is, so to put it, synchronized to NOW; the church is attuned to ETERNITY. The state, by law and power, makes society possible; the church, through the Gospel and the grace of God, seeks the redemption of society.

It follows that wherever the state is willing to be used or can be persuaded to serve as an instrument for that social justice which is a part of the Gospel and the hope of the church for all men but which it cannot and should not itself enforce, then the church should not merely be obedient to the laws by which justice is fortified but give the state its open support and summon the people to full compliance on the level of their individual lives. Moreover, it is the privilege and the duty of religious communities to seek by governmental means the enactment of their ideals and aspirations of human relationships in local and concrete situations; it is theirs to encourage and urge government at all levels to guarantee to all men the rights which belong to all men; it is theirs to seek and to secure, by sheer importunity if by no other means, such legislation as will guarantee to all men the right to have irrespective of superficial and irrelevant distinctions and without the necessity for resorting to violence to secure their rights; it is theirs not only to condemn whatever is

16 H. Richard Niebuhr, *Christ and Culture,* Harper & Brothers, New York, 1951, q.v. for a comprehensive delineation of the roles of church and state and their relationship to each other.

unjust in the law and applaud whatever is just but to be everlastingly insisting that more and more of the stuff that American creeds and dreams are made of be translated into conduct through those instruments of government which fortify justice.

It is axiomatic that social injustice can be obliterated only by changing the systems which tolerate and promote injustice and that the state is the proper instrument through which to make prompt and practical changes in the social order. We conclude, therefore, that the hope of the Negro in America for an end to racial discrimination in our time rests primarily, not in a protracted program which woos the souls of men to good will nor in the coercive pressures which Negroes themselves may bring to bear upon the social order, but in a federal government which is increasingly disposed to establish justice. It is unbecoming of the white church to envy the state's role and neglect its own; and it will be tragic if the white church, as it is now tempted to do, permits its warm sympathies for the feelings and the perplexities of its people to involve it in tactics which obstruct or delay the efforts of the state to make real in society a cardinal part of that Gospel which has been entrusted to the church.

6.

Segregation and
the Right to Belong

---

*There is no caste in blood, which runneth
of one hue; nor caste in tears
which trickle salt withal.*

—BUDDHA

*Of every hue and caste am I, of every
rank and religion.*

—WHITMAN

What determines the morality and the immorality of segregation? Specifically, what primary order, what sacred principle, what will of God is violated by the segregation of the Negro in church and in society? If we are to answer these questions correctly, if we are to see clearly that it is sometimes wrong to separate people from people, then we must see first that it is not always wrong to separate people from people; we have a case against certain forms of segregation only when we see the case for certain forms of segregation.

Therefore, in our search for a criterion by which to judge racial segregation let us remember first that some of the dearest and most beautiful experiences of life require the deliberate, absolute, and permanent exclusion of all other people. Marriage and family life, for examples, are such experiences; and against these exclusive social unities the charge of segregation in its ugly tones is never leveled. It is taken for granted that there are special kinds of unions of life and that the nature of such unions requires the absolute exclusion of those who are not integral parts of them. Segregation, then, the separation of people from people, cannot be condemned as such. There is a love which has the right, the duty, to say "no" to many applicants so that it may say a proper "yes" to some.

Secondly, let us see that the test of the rightness and wrongness of segregation cannot be made by consulting the desires of people. Racial segregation is not evil because the wishes of human beings have been denied or because the range of their lives has been restricted by force. This occurs all the while in a social order, and sometimes such a denial and restriction is legitimate and right and at other times it is illegitimate and wrong. For example, if a society is to be stable there are areas of the life of that society into which people must not be admitted indiscriminately. Society, therefore, prevents the impersonating of officers of the law, the practicing of medicine by those who are not qualified to do so, the marriage of minors. Thus one of the exigencies of social welfare requires that certain people be prohibited from areas of life occupied by other people; to do otherwise is to invite anarchy and jeopardize the common welfare. What the people want, including the desire of the people for unfettered lives, is, consequently, not the test of the morality or immorality of racial segregation.

Finally, we might assume that if this is not the answer it at least suggests where the answer is to be found. It is concluded, in other words, that the evil of racial segregation lies in the fact that it excludes people on the basis of circumstances which are beyond their control. After all, a man does have the possibility of becoming an officer of the law; a student can aspire to the medical profession with reasonable hope; minors do grow up; but racial characteristics are indelible. Dr. Benjamin E. Mays, toward whom many of us have often turned with confidence and respect, has made this point a major argument against racial segregation: ". . . to segregate a man because his skin is brown or black, red or yellow, is to segregate a man for circumstances over which he has no control. And of all the immoral acts, this is the most immoral."[1]

We admit that it is immoral to segregate a man because of his color; but the immorality is not rooted in the fact that his color is beyond his control. Frequently within society people are rightfully separated from other people on the basis of circumstances over which they have no personal control. For example, the insane must for their own good and the good of society be segregated from the sane for the duration of their insanity, and the diseased who have contagious diseases are quarantined. The fact that such people are excluded from the company of other people on the basis of circumstances which they cannot control does not brand that exclusion as immoral. The test by which racial segregation is condemned must evidently be found elsewhere.

These cases which show segregation justified have, however, a most instructive common factor: in each one the segregated are rightfully excluded from that to which they do not belong. The impostor who impersonates an officer of the law, the layman who practices medicine, the minor who pretends that he is of marriage-able age are all excluded from a relationship to which they aspire and they are excluded because they do not qualify; they do not belong. The insane and the infectious are quarantined and thus kept away from the sane and the healthy because they cannot qualify; they do not belong with the sane and the healthy. To cast them entirely beyond the bounds of society, beyond its care and concern, as was done in medieval and ancient times, would be immoral; to

[1] Benjamin E. Mays, "The Moral Aspects of Segregation," published by the Southern Regional Council, republished by *Christian Community* (Evangelical and Reformed Church, Cleveland, Ohio).

segregate them within society is not immoral. The intruder and the stranger are shut from the intimate circle of marriage and family because they are not integral parts of marriage and family; they do not belong.

This indicates that segregation has to do with the right to belong. Union is the relationship of those who belong to each other or who have oneness because they are mutually related to that to which they both belong; segregation is the denial of the right to belong on the basis of irrelevant considerations. It is the breaking of a union which ought to be, on grounds which have nothing to do with the union or with those who should participate in it. The abandoned child, the outcast brother, the neglected parent, the betrayed Lord, the forsaken country—these are spectacles of broken union which carry in them the essence of the evil of segregation. Segregation breaks the union of those who ought to be united by the arbitrary exclusion of the one party by the other. And we are here using the word *ought,* not in the sense of expediency or need, but to connote a primary order of life, an elemental rightness, an eternal will. Segregation is that act, or those acts, which separate a person or persons from those to whom they belong on the ground of circumstances irrelevant to the union which ought to be. Discrimination, in our definition, has to do with the unjust separation of people from things and circumstances; segregation, in our definition, has to do with the immoral separation of people from people. Here, too, as in so many other areas of life, we have depersonalized the problem; we speak of segregated schools, segregated hotels, segregated swimming pools, segregated churches; but what we mean, of course, is segregated people.

Racial segregation falls under this judgment and under no other. It is evil for the simple reason that it severs a person or a people from those to whom they belong on the basis of capricious, arbitrary, and irrelevant considerations of race. In the mind of the segregationist, minor and superficial human distinctions are accounted sufficient to warrant the rupture of major and basic human identities. The Negro is a man but he is prohibited from a free association with other men because of his race and he is thereby excluded from man's estate. The Negro is a citizen and in the civil order all other considerations are secondary to that fact; but he is denied a full participation in the rights of citizenship because of his race and he is thereby cut off from that civil body to which he belongs. The Negro is a Christian, which means that he belongs to the Christian community, to the whole fellowship of those who are one in Christ; but by his color he is kept from communing with some parts of the household of faith and he is thereby barred from a primary union by an incidental distinction. This is the immoral aspect of racial segregation: it denies and violates on the ground of race that human oneness which is obvious in nature, which is proclaimed by the highest order of government, and which is a central doctrine of the Christian religion.

The obvious relationship between discrimination and segregation must now be noted. Discrimination is the impertinent denial of the right to have; segregation is the irrelative denial of the right to belong. Since there are vast areas of life in which you cannot have without belonging, it is plain that segregation usually involves all the evils of discrimination and that it is a most convenient tool for those who, for whatever reason, seek to deprive their fellow man. Whether segregation is an expression of racial pride or merely an absent-minded, habitual observance of custom, it ends in the Negro's losing what is rightfully his by his being excluded from that humanity, that citizenship, or that spiritual community to which he rightly belongs. Segregated schools, buses, playgrounds, hotels, restaurants, churches, etc., are denials not merely of the right to belong but also of the right to have.

But we have given our attention to the problems and to the cures of discrimination and must examine now those evils which would be inherent in segregation even though in keeping certain people apart it still allowed them to have in full what is properly theirs. What can we say to that majority of Americans who believe that the answer to the racial problem is to be found in the establishing of parallel societies which are separate but equal? A surprising number of conscientious American minds, both white and Negro, hold to this view. They do not suggest, of course, as they once did, that these parallel societies occupy separate geographic areas, but they hope that one nation can somehow be made to embrace two distinct societies. To them discrimination is wrong but a segregated social system purged of all discrimination would be right.

So we must ask why it is that a Negro wants his child to attend a white school even though the Negro school is just as good or better. In my home county in South Carolina and in neighboring Clarendon County, where one of the cases which carried to the Supreme Court arose, the schools for Negro children are now in some instances equal or superior to the schools for white children. A fear of desegregation and a desire to delay or outrun court decisions, as well as a conscientious interest in the Negro on the part of some white people, have prompted the equalizing of school facilities. But there are still Negroes who do not want their children to attend these superior but segregated schools. Why? Are they just being "uppity" or is it because they sense in segregated schools a profaning of a deep and sacred right to belong which has nothing to do with inferior, equal, or superior schools? We must ask why Negroes resent their exclusion from membership in white churches. Don't they have good churches and aren't they happier with their own? And if some Negroes are content *to have* whether they *belong* or not, as some of them are, should they be content? What can we say to such questions and to the rather general notion that separate but equal societies, paralleling cultures, would be an eminently just solution to the problems of race in America?

We know, of course, that the supposition is false from the beginning; paralleling societies cannot be just. This is the correct philosophic assumption underlying the Brown *v.* Board of Education decision of the Supreme Court in 1954; segregation on the basis of race deprives a person of constitutional rights even though the " 'tangible' factors may be equal" and even though the Negro himself may have no objection. Moreover, if there were paralleling societies, the floor from which the Negro would have to begin his cultural and economic development and the ceiling to which he could rise would be considerably lower in his restricted racial grouping than they would be in the adjacent white society. But by supposing that such paralleling and equal societies would be just we can determine whether segregation is per se an evil or whether it is evil only when it results in discrimination, taking from people what they have a right to have.

The fundamental fact which denies the hope for Negro and white social orders which are equal to but isolated from each other is that the lives of Negroes and whites are already so thoroughly merged that the separation of the one from the other would be literally impossible. The roots of the histories of Negroes and whites in this country run so deep into a common past and are so intricately intertwined as to be virtually indistinguishable and certainly inseparable. In point of time the Negro is second only to the Indian and the Englishman in claiming America as a homeland, and the Negro arrived only a few years after the Englishman. In patriotism the Negro has a unique honor, being the first to shed his blood for American independence. (It would be interesting to know how many descendants of Crispus Attucks, the ex-slave who was the first to fall in the Boston Massacre in 1770, if he had descendants, have been invited to join the Sons or Daughters of the American Revolution.) Moreover, Negroes and whites are sharers and producers of a common culture. The impact of the white man upon the life of the Negro has been tremendous and dramatic. But there has also been a reciprocal influence, less extensive and deep and less dramatic, perhaps, but nonetheless real; the Negro by his presence on the American scene has had a large part in molding that culture which the white man believes to be entirely his own. The influence of the Negro upon the white man's conventions, his customs, his songs, his language, his accent, his temperament, his religion, has been such that there is no white man in the South today, however "pure" his blood, who is not to some extent culturally a Negro. The whites must count the Negroes among

124

their spiritual ancestors whether they like it or not and the Negroes must acknowledge that in the whites they have the larger part of their cultural paternity. If by some miracle a complete physical separation of the races were effected, we could not in a thousand years undo what we have done to each other.

Indeed, however indelicate the subject may seem to some and however much the racial purists try to ignore the fact, this is true not only spiritually and culturally but also to a degree biologically. The Negro, biologically, is today not genetically the same Negro that landed in Jamestown in 1619, and, with the "passing" of thousands of Negroes into the white community each year, neither is the white man *as a race* genetically the same white man who came to this land a few years earlier. The visible and invisible mixture of the races has been and still is in process. Moreover, the economic lives of Negroes and whites are of one piece. What the prejudiced white man desires psychologically—the annihilation of the Negro—would be disastrous for the white man agriculturally, industrially, and economically. Cut the economic jugular vein of the Negro and the white man bleeds. And, to speak of nothing more, the two races are in the main embraced by a common faith, worship the same God, read the same Bible, endorse the same code of morality, hope for the same heaven, drink the same Cup, and serve the same Lord. This is a broken kinship but it is nevertheless a kinship which is rich in fact and tremendous in possibility. To speak of separating two races which are thus caught up in one bundle of life into separate and paralleling societies is to ignore that long intermixture which has made them one; and to hope that such a separation of the two races could be brought about without doing a deep injury to the body and soul of one race or the other or of both is obviously a delusion. Indeed, Negroes and whites are involved in a biological, cultural, social, economic, and spiritual oneness which cannot be broken.

Therefore, if we may think for a moment in paradoxical terms, segregation in its deeper definition is the separating of that which cannot be separated; in other words, it splits on the circumference of life that which cannot be split at the center. It denies on the edges of human existence that which cannot be denied at the core. Perhaps we can illustrate this thought in the following way. We know that the relationship of mother and baby is one of biological and psychic "belongingness." If mother forsake child or child be kidnapped from mother, their oneness is disturbed at one level but it is not disrupted at another. If the oneness of mother and baby could be completely destroyed, then mother would not mourn for child and child would not cry for mother. The agony, the anxiety, the tension, the sorrow of separation are a result of the fact that a oneness which can never be destroyed has been somewhat destroyed.

Tillich has said that "illness, in the largest sense of body, soul and spirit, is estrangement."[2] This is a beautiful and searching statement from an authoritative theologian; but I must nevertheless add the suggestion that "illness, in the largest sense of body, soul and spirit, is estrangement" from that from which one cannot be estranged. It breaks on the surface a relationship which cannot be broken at the center. Physical illness is alienation from that physical nature from which one cannot escape except in death. Spiritual sickness is flight from a God whose presence is everywhere. Social sickness is alienation from a human union from which one cannot be separated. And, in the train of this thought, racial segregation is a temporal behavior which assumes that it has cancelled the eternal fact of the oneness of man; it separates on the social, or economic, or civil level that which cannot be separated in the deeper reaches of the human soul. And the result for white man and Negro is an illness, the illness of those who are estranged from those to whom they belong. For however fine we may draw out the nerve which connects man to man, it does not break. If it did, all the agonies, the aches and sorrows of human separation would break with it; but it does not break; it holds forever, thin and taut; and along this nerve throb the anxieties, the

[2] Reprinted by permission from the June, 1956, issue of *Pastoral Psychology*. Copyright 1956 by Pastoral Psychology Press, Great Neck, N.Y.

fears, the pangs of human estrangement.

From the anxieties of this separation the white man has in the past tried to escape, not by restoring and completing the broken union, but by seeking to make the severance complete. Said the white man to himself, "If I can debase this creature to a subhuman level, make him one with the beasts of the fields, then these intolerable vexations in my heart and mind will disappear and I shall be at ease." He set his clergy to the task of showing that the relationship between white and Negro is, by divine order, not one of man and man but one of master and servant. He showed through the studies of his anthropologists that there are in the physiognomy of the Negro plain evidences of the mental and physical inferiority of the Negro and even subtle hints that the Negro may be a subspecies midway between man and animal, naturally endowed for hard labor but fitted for nothing else. He declared through his scholars that the mental incapacities of the Negro deny that he is man, saying in the words of John C. Calhoun, "If I could find a Negro who knew Greek syntax, I should believe that the Negro was a human being and ought to be treated as a man." He wrote it into his law, as Justice Taney put it in the Dred Scott case, that the Negroes "had for more than a century . . . been regarded as beings of an inferior order; and altogether unfit to associate with the white race, either in social or political relations; and so far inferior that they had no rights which the white man was bound to respect."[3]

Thus the white man has sought to ease his own vexed spirit by wiping from the table of his memory all records of that oneness in which God has forever bound all of his children. The seat of the white man's misery in regard to the Negro is the fact that he has tried and is still trying to break what cannot be broken, to shatter

[3] Dred Scott *v.* Sanford (1857), 19 How. 393, 15 L.Ed. 691. For this reference I am indebted to Judge Edward F. Waite, who "opened his eyes upon a torn and distracted country when the fires from the *Dred Scott* eruption were kindling civil war" and who died in 1958, dean of all men of good will in the upper Midwest. See: "The Negro in the Supreme Court" by him. 30 *Minnesota Law Review* 219–304, Minneapolis, 1946.

at its center a relationship which he has severed on the surface. It is an embittering and frustrating task, doomed to failure; for the brother whom God has put and keeps in the heart, at the center of all exclusive circles, you cannot with sweet conscience exclude from your life. Three hundred years of failure should have convinced the white man that his poignant uneasiness about his relationship to the Negro has its solution, not in further estrangements of the one from the other, but in a reconciliation which acknowledges on the surface of life that oneness, unbreakable and imperishable, which is the central fact of all human intercourse. The answer to the anxieties of separateness, says Erich Fromm in *The Art of Loving,* "lies in the achievement of interpersonal union, of fusion with another person, *in love.*"[4]

Seen from the Negro's point of view, the anxieties of separateness are different from those apparent in the troubled conscience of the white man. What the white man as the segregator wills to deny, the Negro as the segregated is not permitted to affirm. The white man bears the major guilt of segregation; the Negro bears the major burden of segregation. The white man is in the role of the mother who has willfully forsaken her child; the Negro is in the role of the willfully forsaken child. The mother can but will not return to that oneness which she has flouted; the child would but cannot be restored to that oneness from which it has been expelled. The agonies of the Negro under segregation are the agonies of suffocation; he is cut off from the sources of full life by being separated from that to which he belongs. To be his whole and healthy self he must be able to identify himself in free and complete association with that of which he is a part. To the extent to which the Negro as a man is isolated from being and acting as a man, to the extent that he can think of himself as a citizen but is deprived of the duty and privilege of a citizen, to the extent that he as a spirtual being is denied fellowship in worship and service with those who worship and serve the same God, to that extent he

[4] Erich Fromm, *The Art of Loving,* Harper & Brothers, New York, 1956, p. 18.

lives in a tent in which the oxygen of his being is slowly exhausted and in which he becomes a pallid semblance of his real self. What William Temple said of the unemployed applies even more to excluded Negroes: ". . . they are not wanted! That is the thing that has power to corrupt the soul of any man not already far advanced in saintliness."[5] We shall see in a later chapter what discrimination and segregation do to the human soul, and we are now merely establishing the fact that man has a psychic need to belong to that to which he belongs and that the Negro through racial segregation is cut off from those associations which are indispensable to his being.

The need to belong requires little demonstration; it is the theme of psychological textbooks; forms the plots of novels and dramas; explains the bizarre dress and eccentric speech of adolescents; supports multitudinous fraternities and sororities; promotes church membership, patriotism, mob violence, and class reunions. There are numerous patterns of human behavior which make sense only because of the universal human need to belong. This is well known; but we must be impressed once more by the fact that the urge to belong, even in hermit and recluse, is a dominant and basic urge of the human soul and that its satisfaction is indispensable in the development of wholesome personality. The need to belong is a psychic need—deep, primary, and original. Human beings can tolerate an extraordinary amount of physical deprivation and even a physical separation from people provided that they know themselves to be directly and intimately related to those people or to those associations of people to whom they know that they belong; but sanity and personality are in serious jeopardy wherever people are not allowed to be identified with those communities of humanity of which they know themselves to be part and parcel. Racial segregation seriously jeopardizes the personality of the Negro and is a vicious threat to his mental and moral stability because it is forever thwarting his psychic need to belong to that to which he

[5] William Temple, *Christianity and the Social Order*, a Pelican Series reprint, 1956, Penguin Books, Ltd., Harmondsworth, Middlesex, England, p. 20.

belongs and apart from which he cannot be what by nature, citizenry, and the grace of God he is.

This need to belong, as it affects the Negro, is illustrated by a touching bit of human drama seen some time ago by my wife. Upon moving to West Virginia we had noticed with some puzzlement that it was customary in the public school attended by our son for the young pupils of the early grades to kiss their teacher good-by twice a day, noon and afternoon, when classes were dismissed. We had naturally wondered what the introduction of a new racial element would do to that custom. When integration began in this particular school, it happened that my wife was present and observed the following scene. At noon one of the first-grade white teachers emerged from her class preceded by an attractive Negro boy, the only Negro in her class. She said, "Now you stand there and the other children will join you and you can all march out together." But as the white children filed by, giving their good-by kisses, the Negro boy came back and tried to worm his way toward the teacher; again he was gently taken aside and told, "You wait here and the other children will join you." The teacher returned to the line, receiving farewell hugs and kisses from the pupils of her class. But as she turned to the last child, it was the Negro boy, a wistful and eager look on his face and tiny arms stretched up to give the teacher a hug and a kiss. This time he was accepted and went contentedly on his way. Probably the Negro child knew no heart-felt and irrepressible desire to kiss the teacher; but there was in him an impulsive hunger to do what all the other children were doing and to be one with the members of his class. In the reaching arms of that little boy we have a symbol of the yearning hearts of all peoples who are segregated from that humanity to which they belong.

In 1944, Rayford W. Logan compiled several articles by Negro leaders under the title "What the Negro Wants."[6] The book is an interesting, comprehensive statement of the dreams, the ambitions,

[6] Rayford W. Logan, *What the Negro Wants,* The University of North Carolina Press, Chapel Hill, 1944.

and the intentions of Negro America in its struggle for full manhood and full citizenship. Yet I put the book down with the feeling that one of the primary longings of the Negro soul had not been mentioned by any of the Negro writers. Surely, in addition to things and conditions equal to those enjoyed by white people, *what the Negro wants is to be wanted.* He wants to be gladly accepted into the family of man; he has been the innocent and unwilling Prodigal and now wants to come home to himself and to his brother. This yearning to belong, which has had relatively little expression in the prosaic writings of the Negro, reveals itself in much of his poetry. Here, where his spirit has spoken without shame or restraint, we hear his cry for acceptance by the hearts and lives of other men.

Some years ago in Minneapolis, Minnesota, I sat at lunch with another white man, three Negroes, and the novelist Sinclair Lewis as he gathered insights and material for *Kingsblood Royal.* I have since felt that *Kingsblood Royal* commercialized to some extent the plight and sorrow of the Negro; but Sinclair Lewis had, nevertheless, what was for a white man an extraordinary perception of the racial problem as it appears to the Negro. At one point in the conversation the other white man said, "Wouldn't the Negro be satisfied if . . .," at which point the novelist interjected a quick interruption, "No, no, you can always break off that question, 'Wouldn't the Negro be satisfied if . . .' by saying, 'No, the Negro wouldn't be satisfied!' " This was his way of saying that no temporary, partial, stopgap concession, no Fabian retreat by the white man, will ever satisfy the Negro. He wants all that is his as a man and a citizen and a child of God. Nothing short of that fullness will ever or should ever satisfy the Negro; and that fullness includes the right to belong and the right to be wanted by those to whom he does belong.

It is here that we find the immediate tragedy in the relationship of the two races; for the white man has now taken a determined stand at that door through which the Negro must pass if he is to enter into oneness with his white brother. It is as though the white

131

man were saying, "You can be my equal in things, but you will do it without my help; and however much you may become my equal in possessions, in conditions, in talents, you will not enter into the sanctuaries of my society or into the chambers of my heart." For the ironic fact is that in the past fifty years, as the Negro has risen toward material equality with the white man, he has progressively lost unity with the white man. That is, as he has been gaining equality in the material realm he has been losing equality in its spiritual sense. So far as the material and civil realms are concerned, Negroes and whites are closer together than they have ever been before; that is, they are more nearly on a par with each other. But so far as the realm of brotherhood is concerned they are farther apart; that is, they are more deeply estranged from each other.

This is a trend which Kelly Miller noted exactly forty years ago; he wrote, "The more progressive and ambitious the Negro becomes, the less tolerable he seems to be to his white lord and master. The good old Negro slave who was ever faithful and loyal to the welfare of his lord and master was always acceptable to him. But his more ambitious son, with college diploma in his knapsack, is *persona non grata*."[7] What has been happening in the years which have passed since those words were written confirms their prophetic wisdom. The Plessy *v.* Ferguson decision of the Supreme Court in 1896 has now been reversed by the Supreme Court decision of 1954; but the psychological factors underlying the original decision have not been canceled and continue to motivate the attitude and behavior of whites toward Negroes. If there has been a change, it has merely been a change in accent. The "separate but equal" doctrine has now become in the popular mind an "equal but separate" doctrine. Negroes and whites have grown closer together in similarity of facilities, but they have grown farther apart in the awareness and practice of spiritual identity. It might be said that while the two races have been achiev-

[7] Kelly Miller, *An Appeal to Conscience,* The Macmillan Company, New York, 1918, pp. 16–17.

ing liberty and equality they have progressively lost fraternity. The Negro has come into that day in which at last he is beginning to have, but it is a day in which he cannot yet seriously hope to belong.

To understand this deep and growing rift between the white man and the Negro we must see it in contrast to certain settings in which the Negro has had and still has a relationship of warm personal intimacy with whites. The first illustration takes us once more into ante-bellum days and into those plantation scenes where the Negro slaves, particularly the house servants, often enjoyed an intimate and sometimes mutually affectionate relationship with the inhabitants of the big house. We keep in mind the fact that this was a master-slave relationship which at best debased the personality of the Negro; but we must acknowledge that between the two in the better plantation settings there was sometimes a warmth of genuine devotion, a free and easy sharing of certain areas of life, an ease in conversation, a solicitousness about each other's physical welfare, which began to wane with the abolition of slavery and which has now largely disappeared from the relationships between the races. A number of Negro writers, who could not be accused of being nostalgic about "the good old days" and who certainly would make no defense of slavery—DuBois, for example—have endorsed the fact that there were such warm and intimate relationships between Negroes and whites "before and directly after the war."

Remnants of this vanishing culture are still found, in the North as well as in the South, wherever Negroes have served white people as sharecroppers or as domestic servants over a number of years. Here we find the development of intimacies, loyalties, and affections which puzzle those who expect the relationship of the races to be one of constant tension and friction. Here the white man will champion the Negro before the law even against the claims of some other white man and even in those cases in which the Negro is obviously in the wrong. Here the white man will show what is certainly more than an opportunistic concern for

133

the health of the Negro. Here the Negro, in contests between his employer and other white or Negro people, will be loyal to his employer. Here the Negro will take pride in the affluence of his white employer and make that affluence the subject of personal boasting in conversation with other Negroes. In these settings and where necessity dictates there will be a common use of household facilities; and physical contact, through these facilities or more directly, will be taken for granted. Within limits a Negro nurse, cook, or maid who has been with a white family for a long time is privileged to scold or command the conduct of the children or even advise or pass judgment upon the behavior of the adults.

Of course, what we are describing is paternalism at its very best. Under a paternalistic system, whether it be slavery or some cultural vestige of slavery, there is an underlying assumption of inequality between master and slave or employer and servant. So long as that underlying assumption of inequality is not questioned or violated, so long as the Negro always carries in the back of his mind the knowledge that he is slave or servant, that he is inferior, so long as the relationship in no way blurs the white man's image of himself as master, employer, and superior, the most casual, warm, and personal relationship may develop between the two. Where inequality is assumed and acknowledged, physical separation is not necessary, The Negro is required by the white man to "keep his place." But the Negro's "place" is not really a place but rather a manner and a mood; his "place" is spiritual rather than spatial. If his mood and manner are right, if his mood and manner reveal in him a genuine spirit of subjection, subordination, and dependency, then his place is almost anywhere. In such settings the physical nearness of the Negro is not abhorrent to the white man; all doors open to him if he "knows his place." What is intolerable to the white man is the slightest suggestion on the part of the Negro that the Negro questions the fundamental and underlying assumption of his inferiority. When that happens, as it now does increasingly, the white man must substitute racial distance for racial doctrine in order to reassert his superiority. In a word, the Negro must be accepted on the white man's terms or be segregated from the white man.

Moreover, so long as the relationship is one of *noblesse oblige* on the part of the white man and groveling dependency and humble gratitude on the part of the Negro, the white man will be generous in sharing his material wealth. "My Negroes," he says, "have the best of everything." This, of course, is a gross exaggeration, but the prestige of the white man is often reflected by the manner in which he treats the Negroes dependent upon him. But when the Negro begins to insist upon his rights, to take what is his, depriving the white man of the warming glow of benevolent paternalism, stands upon his own feet, makes his own plea before the law, then the white man detaches himself from the Negro. Segregation is the white man's last resort in maintaining his comforting notions of racial superiority.

Perhaps the Negro is willing at the present time to settle for *having* and will make *belonging* tomorrow's goal; but, however that may be, it is well for the leadership of both races to recognize that while the physical equivalents of Negroes and whites are increasing, the spiritual equivalents are deteriorating and that this may prove to be the real racial danger and problem of our time. For here we have an attack upon man at the highest level of his manhood. All racial discrimination is bad; but the worst discrimination is "that which cramps the noblest powers." A discrimination which robs a people of their substance on the claim of white superiority is bad enough, but a segregation which strikes at that primordial oneness which embraces all men will prove far more tenacious and in the long run more deadly than any kind of physical discrimination.

Some time ago a South African, in a letter to the *Manchester Guardian Weekly*, described the subtle problem which underlies the deep racial cleavages in his country. He said, "Until there is a complete social maturity there will always be mental 'apartheid.' "[8] If the situation in South Africa has been accurately re-

[8] *Manchester Guardian Weekly*, Thursday, May 9, 1957.

ported, it will be some time before men of good will in that country need concern themselves with the problems of "mental apartheid." Giving to the Bantu the elemental substances and dignities due to human beings will for a long time occupy all of their wisdom and energy. But such is not the case in our country. We have arrived, even in the South, at that time when it is not only reasonable but also imperative to take up the problem of "mental apartheid," the problem of spiritual segregation. We have come into that day when the natural, civil, social, and spiritual oneness of the races which is unbreakable at the core must be mended on the surfaces of life. We have come into that day when the essential kinship of the peoples should no longer be denied and suppressed, ignored and flouted, but be given full expression wherever men meet men. We have come into that day when the exile should be welcomed home and the broken family of man united.

7.

Stereotyping and
the Right to Be

---

*If we take people as they are, we make
them worse. If we treat them as if they
were what they ought to be, we help
them to become what they are
capable of becoming.*

—GOETHE

*If you call a man a bug, it means that
you propose to treat him as a bug.
Whereas if you call him a man, it means
that you propose to treat him as a man.
My profession is to study men. Which means
that I must always call men by their name;
always think of them as men; yes, and
always treat them as men. Because
if you don't treat men as men,
they don't behave as men.*

—ALDOUS HUXLEY, Eyeless in Gaza

To understand fully what racial conflict has
done to the Negro, to appreciate the depth and mortality of his
wound, we must add to our thoughts upon prejudice, discrimina-

137

tion, and segregation the analysis of a fourth word, the word *stereo-typing*. This word was popularized by Walter Lippmann in his *Public Opinion* as a term to express mental attitudes which have no referent in actual facts but which are erroneous assumptions. To Lippmann stereotypes were "pictures in our heads" not necessarily of the world as "we should like it to be . . . the word *ideal* is usually reserved for what we consider the good, the true and the beautiful . . . [but of] the kind of world we expect it to be."[1]

In more recent years the word *stereotype* has been applied particularly to the pictures of *people* which we have in our heads, the classifying of people not by facts but by opinions. This word is, therefore, an apt, handy, and welcomed substitute for several cumbersome phrases by which we had sought to describe the evaluating of a group of people by the lowest member of that group or the evaluating of a person by attributing to him the derogatory characteristics assumed to be common to all members of his group. Thus the indicting of the Negro race by attributing to all members of it the frailties and vices which have been observed in a particular Negro—his ignorance, shiftlessness, slovenliness, or delinquency—or the evaluating of a particular Negro by applying to him qualities good or bad which are assumed to be universally true of all members of his race—cheerfulness, laziness, rhythm— is called the stereotyping of the Negro.

We are all acquainted with the numerous ways in which the stereotyping of the Negro saturates American notions about the race and all members of it. Almost without exception the Negro is cast in menial and servile roles in motion picture and television dramas, in advertisements, and in literature. It is the common belief among many white people that all Negroes are sexually immoral; carry concealed weapons; can sing and dance; prefer a diet of pork chops and watermelon; are lazy; love big words, flashy cars, and colorful clothes; are childish, dependent, and superstitious. Such stereotypes are perpetuated in the white man's

[1] Walter Lippmann, *Public Opinion*, The Macmillan Company, New York, 1930, p. 104.

literature, humor, entertainment, advertisements, etc., and these clichés persist despite the exceptions known to almost every white man. There is, for all who are interested, an ample literature on the extent, the effect, and the injustice of the stereotyping of the Negro, a literature which needs no documentation or clinical support from those whose studies are outside the socio-psychological fields. But if we are to pursue a Christian interest in the racial problem, we must see what stereotyping, in addition to and as a part of prejudice, discrimination, and segregation, does to the personality of the Negro and, indirectly, to the soul of the white man.

Let us see first that the stereotyping of the Negro currently takes three forms. Obviously, for one, it is an open and direct debasement of the Negro to a subhuman level, an aggressive, offensive weapon by which prejudice is expressed and segregation and discrimination are justified. If the white man can rationalize his bigotry, maintain his racial advantage in economic and political power, and establish his racial pride by fastening tags of calumny to the Negro and making them stick, he will be strongly tempted to do so. Belief that the Negro is inherently inferior to the white man in moral and mental capacities, that he is naturally criminal, that he is physically equipped to do menial labor and nothing more, that he is indigenously lazy, and that he cannot appreciate the finer things of the white man's culture—including the value of money—such belief is essential to the white man as he exhibits his racial pride and prejudice and as he wields his unjust and exploitative advantage over the Negro. He must degrade the Negro and keep him degraded in order to have the Negro available as a usable material.

Secondly, the stereotyping of the Negro may take the form of faint praise. Here the white man attributes to all Negroes characteristics which are lovable but not necessarily respectable. The essential dignity and nobility of the Negro are concealed, in other words, by applying to the Negro characteristics which seem to praise but actually damn him. The clichés make him a being worthy of the white man's warm, kindly indulgence and affection but not worthy of the white man's admiration and respect. Here the Negro is not respected as an equal human being and a closely related child of God but is loved and indulged as one might love and indulge a pet or a mentally incompetent child. Thus the ignorant, thoughtless, or prejudiced white man says of Negroes, "They're such a cheerful people and so musical. They don't have a worry in the world. Negroes are so carefree and easygoing; they enjoy life." Thus, before the real Negro the white man, believing himself to be generous, fair, and truthful, erects the façade of the Negro as he imagines him to be.

An example of this kind of stereotyping occurred recently in a letter to the *Savannah Morning News*. The writer of the letter, who proposed to give "the viewpoint of progressive and enlightened Southerners," wrote, "Now, I, among many Southerners really like Negroes, (not all of them of course.) I enjoy many of their racial qualities: their native humor and good humor; their sense of rhythm, quaint expressions and lovely voices; and, in those rare ones, their simple humility, true wisdom and deep spirituality."[2] An enlightened Southerner would, of course, recognize immediately that such maudlin tributes are an affront to any intelligent, sensitive Negro. But it is behind such tributes which, with a free hand, the white man bestows upon the Negro that the white man hides the virtue of the Negro as a human being, a citizen, and an image of God.

The third and more recent form in which the Negro is stereotyped is much more subtle but is equally harmful. Here the stereotyping is produced by those who are genuinely interested in the Negro and in the securing of his rights but who have romanticized him. They close their eyes tightly against racial differences which do exist and form, in disregard of the plain facts, a glamourized picture of the Negro. To them every Negro woman is a Marian Anderson and every Negro man is a Ralph Bunche, if not

2 *Savannah Morning News*, Savannah, Georgia, Sunday, March 11, 1956.

actually at least potentially. But, of course, nothing is achieved by portraying Negroes and their conditions as better than they actually are, however much can be hoped for in estimating the Negro's possibilities in a society which did not hamper and restrict his full development. There is no merit in ignoring the factual inequalities of the Negro in his relationship to the white man's achievements in health, education, and the arts. Misrepresentation of these facts and of their sources is, indeed, often adduced as grounds for discrimination and segregation; but it is tragic for sensible people to ignore and even avoid all mention of the facts because those facts have been distorted or for fear that they, too, may by their mention of the deficiencies of Negroes be misunderstood. Solutions of the racial problem which are attempted on the basis of a sentimentalized, romanticized view of the Negro, a view which allows for no discussion of the facts whether they be disagreeable or not, must fail. To pretend that the Negro in general is not only innately and potentially equal to the white man but presently and actually equal to him in his intellectual, moral, and social development is to found racial good will on a witless and deliberate blinking of the facts. And this is to do the Negro a gross disservice. We cannot see the seriousness of the problem until we see the Negro as he is.

It is not discrimination to say that "The Negro suffers most from the diseases of poverty and ignorance, from tuberculosis, syphilis, pneumonia, rickets, and pellagra, and so forth."[3] It is not discrimination to say that the Negro's level of literacy is beneath that of the white community, that his infractions of the law are out of proportion to his population, if we make such statements in the recognition of statistically documented facts and do so to help rather than to hurt the Negro. The erroneous interpretations of such facts, interpretations which attribute to the facts sinister explanations in terms of a subhuman and sub-

[3] R. M. MacIver, *The More Perfect Union,* The Macmillan Company, New York, 1948, p. 38.

141

moral nature for the Negro, are, of course, a blatant and irresponsible racism; but the escape from the dilemmas of racial conflict must not be by way of a flight from reality.

The Negro and the white man both have cause to be ashamed of the facts—the white man more, the Negro less. But it is with the facts, with the Negro as he is, that all sound programs for the solving of the racial problem must begin. And if we are to see the Negro as the Negro is, then in all our appraisals of him we must make allowance for the same latitude of indolence, indifference, avarice, hatred, prodigality that we find in the white man. The Negro, too, is not merely a creature caught "in the fell clutch of circumstance." For him, of course, there is a victimizing history over which he has little control; but he, too, can be something more than the product of social forces. For Negro leaders and their white supporters to make apologies for that Negro who is less a man than he can be is in effect to rob the Negro of that sense of personal integrity by which he is responsible for himself before his God. The Negro as a noble savage, innocent and blameless, is a myth which the Negro should abhor and resist even as he does any other stereotyping of his personality. If the romantic friends of the Negro should have their way and convert us all to this beatific stereotyping of the Negro, we should then assume that all is right with the Negro's world and complacently retire, leaving him to the titles of his grandeur and to the facts of his misery.

This much about stereotyping is generally known, but it is sometimes difficult for the white man to understand why the educated and sensitive Negro resents stereotyping in all of these forms even more than he does discrimination and segregation. Why, asks the white man, should the Negro be so touchy about pictures of a buxom, bandannaed Aunt Jemima on a box of pancake flour; why is he abashed by Stepin Fetchit, Rochester, and Amos and Andy; why does the spirit curdle in him when he sees the lawns of white people decorated with statues of little Negro boys serving as imitation hitching posts; why does he blanch when a white person, or a Negro, tells a joke which involves one of the clichés about the Negro? Is he hypersensitive? Is this a measure of the depth of his insecurity? Or is something even more perilous to him involved here?

I suggest that the keen-minded, alert Negro senses in the stereotyping patterns the symbol of the white man's ultimate assault upon the personality of the Negro. I suggest that in the stereotyping of the Negro there is epitomized the final invasion of the last sanctuary of the human soul—a man's right to be. It is good to have; but there is something more precious in life than having. It is good to belong; but there is something more fundamental to life than belonging. Beneath the right to have lies the right to belong; beneath the right to belong lies the right to be. The highest and deepest cry of the soul of man is not "Let me have!" nor "Let me belong!" but "Let me be!" Stereotyping is the symbolic denial of the right to be.

If we say that all Negroes are as bad as any Negro and that no Negro is ever any better than all Negroes, we have in effect said that there is no such thing as *a* Negro. Stereotyping denies the Negro as a unique, individual, and irreplaceable person. It is the denial of individuality; it is the refutation of the sacredness of personality. By degrading the race to the level of the lowest individual and by degrading the highest individual to the level of the race we rob the Negro of his genius, his genuineness, and his originality. By the use of stereotyping we thoroughly depersonalize him; we make all Negroes alike, reasonable facsimiles one of the other, undistinguished by individual marks. To us they are all the same thing endlessly repeated. Cite some exceptionally able and successful Negro to the rabid racist and he will reply, "He's still a nigger," as though the fact of race were a disgrace leveling and equalizing all Negroes. We may therefore use the word *stereotyping* to symbolize the destruction of the Negro as a person under the impact of discrimination and segregation. It epitomizes the denial of the Negro's right to be. The alert, sensitive Negro is wise, then, in directing his primary resentment, not against those who hurl sticks and stones but against him who filches his good name.

We must not brush this thought aside as though it were a sentimentalizing of the racial problem, insisting that we must consider more practical issues: jobs, votes, and so forth. For here, indeed, we begin to touch the problem of racial oppression at its most vital center, and we have skimmed the surface of it unless we look at the oppressions which the racial struggle inflicts not only upon the Negro's possessions, his right to have; not only upon the Negro's associations, his right to belong; but also upon the fibers of his soul, his right to be.

Here we find that the social psychologists have done an immense amount of most satisfactory and convincing study and we need only to refer to their findings. We can do so in a few swift quotations and examples. Segregation and discrimination cause the Negro "severe mental anguish and panic . . . paroxysms of shifting emotions . . . produce a collapsing effect upon the individual's self-respect . . . ashamed of his existence."[4] "Self-hatred is common to most minorities. . . . He accepts all the stereotypes about his people uncritically."[5] "The systematic subordination of Negroes to white people in the American social system has a definite effect upon the development of Negro personality."[6] We could thus quote at some length from a variety of works which show how the souls of Negroes are assaulted by the racial patterns.

A thorough study of the effects of racial oppression upon the personality of the Negro is given in *An American Dilemma* under the chapter entitled "The Protest Motive and Negro Personality."[7] Myrdal and his associates in this chapter tell how and

[4] Oliver Cromwell Cox, *Class, Caste, and Race,* Doubleday and Company, Garden City, N.Y., 1948, p. 383.
[5] Alfred J. Marrow, "Living Without Hate," Harper & Brothers Publishers, New York, 1951, p. 90–91.
[6] W. Lloyd Warner, *Color and Human Nature,* American Council on Education, Washington, D.C., 1941, p. 6.
[7] Gunnar Myrdal, *An American Dilemma,* Harper & Brothers, New York, 1944, Chapter 36.

why the Negro develops what is called "the Negro inferiority complex"; describe the Negro's temptation to self-pity on the one hand and a "cynical disregard for 'the rules of the game' when dealing with white people" on the other hand; point out that the Negro is apt to develop a dual personality, being self-assertive in dealing with other Negroes and self-accommodating in dealing with whites; explain the urge upon the Negro to give violent expressions to his sense of futility and frustration; and indicate that the Negro's "attitude of carefree complacency" is actually a "complacency tinted with much bitterness." Of these perils to Negro personality one, especially dangerous to the soul of the Negro, is the temptation to shift the blame for failure and disappointment from personal inadequacy to the racial system and those who support it. The Negro who can find satisfaction in this excuse has a convenient escape from responsibility. And this, of course, is a poisonous draught, lulling the Negro into indolence and passivity, deadening ambition, and dissipating those energies by which some sense of personal worth could be achieved. The perennial task for the Negro is, on the one hand, that of evading that sense of personal and racial inferiority which a prejudiced white culture encourages and to which he is tempted to acquiesce in moments of fatigue and, on the other hand, that of avoiding that projecting of blame to which all men are liable and to which a harassed race is particularly vulnerable. "The temptations are great, however, to lose this precious balance, either by falling into the bitter complacency of the inferiority doctrine . . . or by overdoing the equality doctrine and trying to build up a strained case that black is superior to white. A third temptation is to exaggerate the accusation against the whites and so use the caste disabilities to cover all personal failures."[8] These are sufficient references to show that the soul of the Negro, in the opinion of sociologist and psychologist, is continuously in multiple jeopardy under the harassments of race pressures or, to say it in our terms, that the right of the Negro to be is in continuous peril.

[8] *Ibid.*, p. 760.

145

"Ask yourself," said Gordon W. Allport, "what would happen to your own personality if you heard it said over and over again that you were lazy, a simple child of nature, expected to steal, and had inferior blood. Suppose this opinion were forced on you by the majority of your fellow-citizens. And suppose nothing that you could do would change this opinion because you happen to have a black skin."[9] The anxiety, the uncertainty, the nervous strain which accompany a Negro whenever he enters a store, a restaurant, a movie, a park, a hotel, a white church, are traumatic in their effect upon his personality. Unless he can make a psychic adjustment which he can hold in dignity, life becomes for him a daily humiliation. The word of the white man, the thought of the white man, the deed of the white man, the pressures of the white man's world—these take a man who is born a Negro and make him, as Richard Wright would put it, into a "nigger" if they can and when they succeed blame him for it. This point is skillfully and convincingly dramatized in *Native Son*. As the lawyer concludes his defense of Bigger Thomas, he rises to this indictment of society: "This Negro boy's entire attitude toward life is a *crime!* The hate and fear which we have inspired in him, woven by our civilization into the very structure of his consciousness, into his blood and bones, into the hourly functioning of his personality, have become the justification of his existence."[10]

All of this is implied in our statement that stereotyping is the symbolic denial of the Negro's right to be. Stereotyping is, of course, in itself a real denial of that individualism and integrity which are the essence of personality; but, more than that, it is the word which identifies the destructive effects of discrimination and segregation upon the soul of the Negro. In its many forms it works triple tragedies.

First, it is the screen behind which the white man hides in bad

[9] Gordon W. Allport, *The Nature of Prejudice*, The Beacon Press, Boston, 1954, p. 142.
[10] Richard Wright, *Native Son*, Grosset & Dunlap, New York, 1942, p. 335.

conscience or in fearful pride the real Negro. The white man, crass as men can be, could not day by day, year after year, face what he has done to the body and spirit of the Negro; so he must do that one thing more and put the Negro away. The continuously employed and infinitely varied clichés about the Negro enable the white man to do this, to use the word *Negro,* or its less polite variants, and in doing so to have in mind a referent which is identical, not with the real Negro, but with that comforting fiction which the white man has invented. By the use of the stereotype, however harmless it may seem to him, he has made the Negro vanish. Every day, at work, on the streets, in the shops and stores, he meets a man who isn't there. It has been remarked by a number of writers that the Negro as a scapegoat and as exploitable material has a high degree of visibility. This is true; but the real Negro—the Negro as a man, a citizen, a spiritual being, a divine possibility, a person, a "Thou"—has for most Christians a high degree of invisibility. We look at him but we do not see him. We look at him and we see labor or market, tool or stepping stone, color or a flattering contrast to self; but we do not see him. It is a strong expression, but it is no exaggeration to say that many white people in stereotyping the Negro are committing a psychological annihilation of the Negro; they are trying to bury the intolerable fact of the Negro.

We saw earlier that discrimination is not always deliberately malicious. We may say also that the stereotyping of the Negro is not always a premeditated plot against his integrity but can be at times nothing more than the reflex action of a traditionally and socially conditioned nervous system. You refuse to "mister" a Negro, not because you despise him or desire to insult him, but simply because you have slowly and unknowingly absorbed an atmosphere which prohibits the giving of gentle titles to Negroes. It requires deep digging into the memory for a Southerner, as this one knows, to recall that time when he first learned that a Negro can be called "uncle" but not "mister," that a Negro woman can be referred to as a woman but never as a lady, that ordinary politeness, to say nothing of the niceties of etiquette, are not required in dealing with colored people.

And acts of suppression, as well as words, even though they may be cruel and insulting to the Negro, are not necessarily motivated by a malicious cruelty and contempt. You refuse the Negro the use of your front door, not always because you want to bemean him and hurt his feelings by denying him status, but simply because to let a Negro enter your home by the front door "just isn't done." The Negro woman can enter into the most intimate and personal relationships with the white home—make the beds, prepare and serve the food, nurse the baby—but she must not enter through the front door, eat at the family table, or expect to be greeted with a title of respect. This, of course, does not make sense; but that is the point. Many of the racial taboos which debase the personality of the Negro have no rhyme or reason, no practical effect, no logic, and no premeditation; they may be no different in intent from those equally thoughtless words and gestures by which we show courtesies to those of our own color. Many of the social acts are entirely mechanical and do not necessarily reveal either an intended courtesy or a deliberate insult. But the result of such quiet and conventional stereotyping is that the Negro as a unique, irreplaceable person gradually vanishes from the mind and heart of the white man.

But stereotyping in this inclusive sense of the word is twice cursed; it curses "him that gives and him that takes." Therefore, the second tragedy of the stereotyping of the Negro is the effect it has upon the white man. Let us consider one practical illustration of the debilitating effect which the stereotyping of the Negro has had upon the white man. In his autobiography, *Up From Slavery,* Booker T. Washington in a very penetrating insight warned the white South that if it required literacy and property holding from the Negro as a qualification for the voting franchise and did not make these same requirements of the white man, then the Negro in meeting these requirements would advance intellectually and materially and the white man would decline. His prediction has not been precisely fulfilled, but the philosophy of it has proved generally true. Without question the rise of the Negro in the South has been at a much more acute rate of ascendancy than the simultaneous rise of the white man. This has been partly due to the fact that the Negro in the past fifty years started so much lower than the white man and had so much farther to climb. But it has also been due to the fact that the white man has had in his midst a "contrast person" with whom, however miserable his own circumstances, he could compare himself favorably. Nothing has been so much a cultural drag upon the white man as has been his low opinion of the Negro. The most illiterate, backward white man, being able to look at the most advanced Negro with the contemptuous thought, "He's a nigger," has been consoled and encouraged in his indolence and reconciled to his low estate. "Free, white, and twenty-one" has been a proud slogan but it has also been the bane of cultural and material progress in the South. In his opinion of the white man the Negro has had the stimulants of challenge; in his opinion of the Negro the white man has had the depressants of consolation.

But, as has been implied already, the most tragic and ironic result of stereotyping is not that it makes the Negro invisible to the white man and that it makes the white man the less human, but that such oppressions have the power to make the Negro invisible to himself. This, to be sure, is by no means universal among members of the Negro community and we shall after a time refer to the surprisingly numerous incidences of remarkably sturdy personalities among Negro people. But it is true, nevertheless, that the social pressures have developed in many Negroes a contempt for their own color and racial characteristics, for proof of which we need only read in magazines printed primarily for a Negro clientele the many advertisements which capitalize upon the Negro's urge to flee from racial identity or analyze the development within Negro communities of class distinctions on the basis of color shadings. The white man's culture, whatever weaknesses this fact may reveal in the Negro, must take the blame for making many Negroes despise rather than cherish what God has made them. Nor can the average Negro listen continuously to those multitudinous voices which shout and whisper interminably that the Negro is intellectually, emotionally, physically, and morally inferior without concluding after a time that perhaps "black is bad." And where the whole social order from top to bottom is rigged against him it is difficult for the Negro to escape the conclusion that perhaps something is naturally wrong with him. How can he, indeed, in such a setting preserve a true picture of himself?

The collapse of Negro personality under the pressures of stereotyping is, of course, not inevitable; but when it does occur it should not be surprising. Douglas Dales in a special report to the *New York Times* stated that "The Chicago Housing Authority disclosed that four Negro families in Trumbull Park Homes had been permitted to move this month to another housing project after physicians had certified that they could no longer stand the tension of living in Trumbull Park."[11]

The task of maintaining a sense of personal integrity is especially acute for the Negro in that climate where he experiences a genteel and conventional stereotyping by the white man. Under open and ruthless oppression he would know his dangers, but here the average Negro does not know what is happening to him, so slow, so soft, so imperceptible are the envelopment and the strangulation of his personality. Like the victim of radiation, he is slowly poisoned and does not know until too late, if at all, how deadly are the invisible blows to his being. The Negro in this setting may, for example, join that large but rapidly diminishing group of Negroes who take the patterns of segregation and discrimination for granted; who assume that this is the order of things and that the Negro's place is properly subordinate to that of whites; who make a smooth, unprotesting, but spiritually debilitating adjustment to the system into which they are born; who

11 *New York Times,* Sunday, August 18, 1957, p. 79.

believe because of a long history of slavery, oppression, and enforced ignorance that the Negro is really inferior to white people and that the black man's role, by the very nature of life, is secondary to the white man's. When he does, his groveling before white people is not merely a conniving way to wheedle favors from them but a genuine reflection of an actual loss or lack of manhood.

But there are also, and in growing numbers, those alert, sensitive, self-respecting Negroes who know what the soft pressures of an apparently harmless and decorous discrimination and segregation are doing to them and to their people. To them persecution is better than paternalism, and the open insult is better than that indifference which rejects them as human beings. Since the sensitive, self-conscious human soul normally would rather be hurt than ignored, hostility toward the Negro has for him at least the value of dignifying his existence, whereas indifference slowly destroys his sense of being. Therefore the Negro, caught in "the moving box" of such a social setting, has these perilous alternatives: flight, duplicity, an increasingly bitter sense of futility, or violent and suicidal rebellion. Nothing in such a situation can prevent the collapse of personality and insure stability of soul, unless the Negro be given or make for himself the opportunity to express the deep yearnings of the race and to strive, unhampered by law and custom and with some hope for success, for the dignities and rights which belong to all people. Such an urge toward human dignity and self-respect is now so widely diffused among Negroes in all parts of the United States, is now so well defined, so self-conscious, so strong, that attempts to repress it in any part of the country will inevitably build up in the Negro explosive pressures which can be controlled neither by him nor by the white community.

We have now seen in sufficient detail that discrimination, segregation, and stereotyping have a deadening effect upon the personality of the Negro, injuring his soul in fact as well as in the mind of the white man and in the Negro's awareness of himself. We have used the word *stereotyping* to gather up in one term all those personal and social forces which destroy the integrity of the

Negro as a human being and deny his right to be. We have stressed the fact that this is, whether the individual Negro knows it or not, the most ominous of all forms of racial oppression. It not only threatens the physical life of the Negro and those associations which are necessary for wholeness but shakes the very ground of his being. Here for the Negro is that one who "after he hath killed hath power to cast into hell." Stereotyping we define, then, as symbolizing the denial of the right to be. Specifically we have said that the stereotyping of the Negro is fundamentally a denial of his uniqueness, his individuality, and his irreplaceableness as a sacred and worthy human being. And we have said that this denial of the right to be is at once the most subtle and the most diabolical of all those foes set against the Negro in American society.

Part Three
The Bonds of Unity

8.

Of One Blood

. . . Till the world is wrought
To sympathy with hopes and fears it heeded not.

—SHELLEY

It is a privilege of man to love even
those who do him wrong. One can reach
this level by reflecting that all men are
of one family with oneself; that their
shortcomings are due to ignorance, and
against their will; that in a short time
both of you will be dead.

—MARCUS AURELIUS

What is the Christian reply to discrimination, segregation, and stereotyping? What attitudes are implied and what behavior is indicated by the Christian answer to racial oppression and racial hostility? On what grounds does the Christian ethic champion the right to have, to belong, and to be? To what bond does Christianity look for the reconciliation of estranged races? The answers to these questions cannot be given in a single and comprehensive pronouncement but must be set forth in three distinct forms which meet the needs of three separate yet overlapping areas of human relationships: what all men owe to all men, what all Christians owe to all men, what all Christians owe to all Christians.

It is obvious that there are Christians whose racial behavior does not rise to the level of the common morality of secular society. If there is a unique Christian communion, they live outside of it and even violate the common decencies which men owe to men. Even as these words are being written there come to hand leaflets which are being widely circulated in the South, condemning desegregation under such titles as "A Southern Christian Looks at the Race Problem" and "Should Christians Support Integration?" These leaflets do not, it must be said, represent the best or the official religious opinions of the South on questions of race; yet they do have a wide circulation. We find that such propaganda, far from being Christian, suggests a philosophy and a program of race relations which fall short of the elemental claims put upon our human relationships by the psychic and physical kinship of all men.

Indeed, the racial problem in America is chiefly one in which Christians are divided from Christians by prejudice, oppression, and racial hostility; and it is a problem to which white Christians are among the principal contributors. Our purpose in giving a triple reply to questions about the solution of racial tension is not, therefore, to set Christian and secular behavior over against one another in odious comparison. It is a plain fact that there are non-Christians who in their interpersonal practices put many Christians to shame. Our purpose is to ask on what grounds and by what motivation they do so.

Nevertheless, when the Christian reply to racial tension is given and the Christian appeal for racial harmony is presented, they must meet the requirements of three distinct but superimposed areas of human relationship: what all men owe to all men, what all Christians owe to all men, what all Christians owe to one another. It is folly to lay against a secular society the ultimate claims of the Christian ethic or to appeal in that society to an authority which it does not recognize or to a bond which in its secular state it cannot experience. It is also wasteful to demand of Christians nothing more than elemental human decency and thus to discredit the quality and the reconciling power of that unity which Christians have in Christ. Therefore, in this and the two succeeding chapters we shall apply the Christian ethic to the specific requirements of each of these three areas of human relationships.

The first of the three areas is that large segment of society which is not consciously motivated or influenced by Christian precepts or the Christian spirit. (We must use the phrase *not consciously motivated* to cover the fact that men who try to write a code of human decency without recourse to those eternal values upon which Christianity relies are inevitably influenced by that faith against which they rebel or to which they are indifferent.) The Christian religion cannot be indifferent to the racial problem in this area, should not leave it to merely humanitarian civilizing influences, and must not surrender it to the charlatan or the racist. On the contrary, the Christian religion has an ethical injunction that it must hold against a society which is secular but for which it is the primary spiritual guardian. Here, however, the Christian ethic finds itself restricted by the limitations of the people to whom it would address its claim. The threshold of its own radical morality is too high for those who do not have the stimulations of its doctrine and its spirit. Therefore, in this area the Christian ethic must cite those denominators of morality which are common to the secular order; it must say, in the main, what it is that all men owe to all men; and it must appeal to the elemental and minimal kinship of all men.

What, then, can the Christian ethic say to a racially divided secular society? At what level can it co-operate with the non-religious yet civilizing forces in society—education, democracy, the state, the humanities, the social sciences—in achieving a just and peaceful social order in which all men have their rightful place and part irrespective of their race, religion, or class? What residual message of human solidarity does it share with the non-

Christian religions and with the secular humanities when all doctrinal dissimilarities have been eliminated and their common claim has been distilled? What bond of human unity pierces the broadest areas of human relationship and speaks to the largest number of people? Is there one touch of nature which makes the whole world kin and is there any healing in that touch?

There is a beautiful pathos in the yearnings of those modern writers who, like Albert Camus, have sought the dignity which belongs to all men and the reconciliation of estranged men "without the aid of eternal values."[1] We cannot say that "they especially" but we can say that "even they" find a ground for good will among men. Within the bounds of the least metaphysics, which is for them the bounds of all that is possible, they find a ground on which men may in dignity and with purpose live and die for one another. But when they say that "man's love for man can be born of other things than an arithmetic calculation of interests or a theoretical confidence in human nature,"[2] we are compelled to ask to what other things they are referring. If the humanitarianism which they propose must be atheistic in its motivation, a kind of non-Christian good will, where do we find the dynamics for such good will?

Some of their answers are bizarre; for example, there is that one which suggests that where men have no God and know it, their love must be lavished on the human race. But such a love often finds its object, not in the human race, but in the particular race, in itself, or in household pets, or in mammon. It is ridiculous to imply that the atheist is the one who necessarily loves man best because he is the one who wastes none of his love on God. Moreover, some of the answers, although they decry "an arithmetic calculation of interests," propose nevertheless that we find the highest promptings for good will among men in the mutuality of human misery. We are, they say, urged to love one another by the great "collec-

[1] Albert Camus, *The Myth of Sisyphus,* Alfred A. Knopf, New York, 1955, Preface.
[2] Albert Camus, *The Rebel,* Alfred A. Knopf, New York, 1954, p. 24.

tive unhappiness" of mankind. This is certainly a more appealing language than that used by Sumner; but it calls for nothing more than that "antagonistic cooperation" which, according to Sumner, bridges the gap between men in their time of mutual peril. Surely we have often seen among men who disclaim religion a good will toward all men which is based neither upon the absurd idea that atheism conserves human love for its rightful object nor upon a crass utilitarianism in which a man for his own sake loves his fellow man. And there are those who have found what is for them a wholly satisfactory secular trail leading through the vast and entangling barriers of racial antagonism. We are asking, then, what is this least ethic which claims the love of man for man.

Let us declare at once that the claim for racial harmony which a racially divided secular society will tolerate from the Christian ethic is at once Christianity's minimal declaration of human unity. For that claim is to nothing more than the elemental biological identity of all human beings. Where the anthropologists conclude—at the primary physical oneness of all men—there the Christian definition begins; what is for the biologists a valid summary serves the Christian solely as a necessary premise; the last word which the sciences of the human organism speak about the oneness of man—his physical relatedness—is but the first syllable in the Christian doctrine of human oneness; and the final appeal of the nonreligious yet civilizing forces in society—an appeal to basic kinship—is merely the preamble of the Christian appeal to a bond which transcends both physical dissimilarity and biological identity. Paul's ingratiating declaration of the elemental physical kinship of all men, that introductory word which he spoke to his Athenian listeners, is frequently cited by Christians as the specific rebuke of human division and conflict; actually, it belongs here, where the Christian ethic again confronts a "Greek" society and not, as it is so frequently and thoughtlessly used, in the vocabulary of those who speak for Christian community.

Even so, all men are biologically equivalent. God has indeed "made from one every nation of men to live on all the face of the earth."[3] The essential biological homogeneity of all people is a fundamental fact which has both religious and scientific confirmation. The Bible and anthropology are both committed to the monogenistic rather than the polygenistic theory of the origin of man. Both recognize that the physical differences between the races are insignificant when compared to the physical identities. This, then, is a generally accepted truth upon which we can set our minimum appeal for the end of racial hostility: all men are members of the same human family and owe to one another the recognition and the practice of that kinship.

To be sure, a mere knowledge of this biologically and Biblically confirmed fact is not enough. The bitterest and most complex problems of human antagonism are not solved by knowledge, not even by the knowledge of closest physical kinship; most human strife, as a matter of fact, is knowingly fratricidal. Therefore, only as the elemental and universal human kinship is translated into a vital emotional experience of that kinship does it become meaningful in the lessening of racial tension. The recognition of physical kinship is academic and meaningless unless it be elevated into the realm of some kind of spiritual affinity.

It is claimed by some sociologists that a coerced change in the racial patterns, one that places the hostile racial groups into new settings of relationship, will, however artificial, improve the racial attitude and behavior of those involved. This is a deceptive half-truth. When people who are antagonistic to one another and who are motivated by no common sense of kinship are compelled to associate with one another, there is provided a setting in which hostilities may either diminish or increase. What happens depends partially on the nature of the new social setting but largely on the hope, the spirit, and the will of the people involved. "Physical proximity without spiritual affinity" can be disastrous, particularly in the field of race relations. Where elbows touch and hearts do not the opportunities for malice and violence are greatly multiplied. For example, the mutual occupation of certain areas by

[3] Acts 17:26b.

Negroes and whites on a free and equal basis—jobs, schools, pools, and parks—may meet the simplest demands of justice but may at the same time rub raw the wounds of racial division.

This means that all meetings of the races are dangerous if they are spatial without at the same time being at least somewhat spiritual. Therefore, desegregation can be viewed as progress toward human harmony only if it is seen as the penultimate stage in human relationships, a stage where the demands of racial justice are met whatever may happen to racial peace, but, nevertheless, a stage which is dangerously occupied if it is considered permanent and final. The gains of desegregation are always themselves in jeopardy unless racial progress is moving beyond desegregation toward integration, beyond animal equality toward the spiritual expressions of the basic animal oneness.

The Christian ethic must continuously remind the secular society, in concert with all civilizing agencies holding this conviction, that the equal sharing of a common space and a common substance by the races does not satisfy the larger claims of the human family. The basic state of human kinship does not declare that all men are equal or that all men should have the same substance—however important that may seem to some. What it does declare is that men, however unequal they may be, *are one substance*, a substance which declares itself in infinite variety.

Erich Fromm, in *The Art of Loving,* has done us all an immeasurable service in showing how the word *equality* has degenerated in our time. He points out that whereas it once implied a relationship of person to person, a relationship of good will and acceptance, it now refers exclusively to the relationship of a person to some thing or condition, a relationship of impersonal justice. He says, "Equality today means 'sameness,' rather than 'oneness.' "[4] Dr. George D. Kelsey has also called to account the loose usage which we are currently giving the word *equality*. He remarks upon the glib manner in which we have accepted "equality

[4] Erich Fromm, *The Art of Loving,* Harper & Brothers, New York, 1956, p. 15.

of opportunity" as the "American Way" in race relations when actually it is "little more than a fiction because it has proposed equality of opportunity without equality of person. . . . It fails to take into account the spiritual and psychological quality of life."[5]

An equality which levels the lives of persons but leaves those persons in isolation from each other may solve for each the problem of things, but it does not touch the problem of their divided oneness. That being true, it is easy for a secular society to concentrate its energies upon the task of securing equality for the Negro and by-pass or ignore altogether that segregation which keeps the human family divided. The Christian ethic, appealing only to its least word, must remind the secular society that something more is at stake than the Negro's right to earn, to dwell, to eat, to play, to live unhindered by those who despise his color or profane his race. It is not enough to give the Negro all these things and yet keep him outside that broad kingdom of spiritual affinity which all men as members of the same human family should share with one another.

We have seen, however, that desegregation, the merely physical association of the races on the level of "sameness," threatens to become for the fatigued part of the Negro leadership and for most of their white sympathizers an end in itself. We have noticed in the American social order a trend which finds the physical segregation of the races lessening but the spiritual segregation of the races increasing. In geometric metaphor we can say that as the peripheries of Negro and white life have moved closer together, the centers of Negro and white life have moved farther apart. Negroes are beginning to use the verb *to have* in its present tense; but the verb *to belong* is for them largely limited to the future tense. Desegregation, equality in relationship to things, increases; integration, an equation in persons, declines. Mutuality and com-

[5] George D. Kelsey, "The Ethico-Cultural Revolution in American Race Relations," *Religion in Life,* Abingdon Press, Nashville, Tenn., Summer, 1957, p. 341.

munication between individual members of the two races are poorer now than they have been at any time in the past half-century.

Among those white people who have grudgingly conceded that desegregation in the public schools is both just and inevitable there are many who believe that the loss of mutuality and communication between the races must and will accompany any reduction of the physical distance between them. We cannot refute the selected facts to which they point: desegregation of the races and estrangement of the races have been concomitant; gains in liberty and equality for the Negro have been matched by losses in fraternity for the Negro. For example, where the public schools have been recently desegregated, as in West Virginia, there has also been a suspension of those social affairs—parties, outings, dances—which had theretofore been a cherished part of the extracurricular life of the students. And this social separation of the white students from their Negro classmates has been due not only to parental edict but also to a reluctance on the part of the white students to enter into commingling social relationships with their Negro fellow students. Meanwhile, sororities and fraternities, normally discouraged by school authorities, have flourished as a segregating device within the desegregated schools. The clinical significance of such instances is indicated when we place them against a background in which desegregation of the schools has proceeded with extraordinary smoothness and almost without incident.

But the present decline of mutuality and communication—however stubborn and pernicious the fact of it may be—is subject to several valid interpretations. Obviously, for one explanation, it is the result of the white man's retreat into that spiritual aloofness which is his last citadel of superiority. Again, it is the result of the Negro's lately gained strength; aware of his legal rights, adept in the use of the instruments which can enforce those rights, alert to his political power, the Negro is no longer dependent upon the sympathies and good wishes of his white friends. That warm, close association with the white man which the Negro in his weakness purchased at the cost of great humiliation is now somewhat expendable. Moreover, we must say of the emotional estrangement of the races that it is, on the white man's part, a normal sociological recoil from the legislative and judicial decisions which have in the past thirty years disturbed the previously unjust but accepted equilibrium of the races. It will require much more time than has passed since the first impact of these recent decisions for the white man to adjust to the new status of the Negro and to the effect of the Negro's new position upon the white man's dominant role in American society. There may, indeed, be still further deteriorations in the spiritual phase of race relations before mutuality and communication begin to return.

However we may explain the worsening of mutuality and communication between the races within the secular world, this is a condition which must be viewed as intolerable by those who believe that physical oneness should evolve into spiritual affinity. Some may be willing to settle for justice between the races; others may conclude that an impersonal desegregation of the races is the highest good that can at present be realistically pursued by men of good will; but those who find a spiritual bond for the races in their shared physical oneness must view the alienation of man from man as a breaking of the wholeness, the oneness of the human family. Their program will therefore involve not merely the securing of justice for all men but even more the recognition and the practice of a fundamental kinship which erases or ignores the secondary characteristics of race. Their program involves conversation, not merely in the perfunctory sense of a pleasant and polite exchange of greetings, but in the archaic meaning of the word *conversation:* an abiding of the one in the other.

For most Americans this, unfortunately, is an end toward which they can move now only in the simplest and most elemental beginnings. Even for those people whose lives are submerged in social settings where Negroes are predominant in number—indeed, especially for them—there is seldom a single relationship of

Negro and white which is an unadulterated relationship of man to man. The patterns of the social order take priority over and literally obscure the relationships of one member of the human family to another. Seldom does white or Negro recognize and greet the other primarily and pre-emptively as fellow man. Until there can be such a meeting of Negroes and whites, a meeting on the fundamental level of what man owes to man apart from the titles and calumnies of custom and the social order, there can be no hope for the end of that fratricidal strife which violates the basic kinship of all men.

Even in the area of secular society there is a portion of the racial problem for which force, any amount or kind of human might, will prove completely futile and for which men must find a bond beyond the law. Justice, at best, in our definition, is a social catharsis, and force, of one kind or another, is its active agent. It can do much, and we have seen that there is much that it should do. But there is much that needs to be done in the racial encounter which justice cannot do. It can put Negroes and whites into physical proximity to one another—on the same buses, in the same schools, restaurants, hotels, etc.— but it cannot restore the broken kinship. Justice can make Negroes and whites share the same space, but no amount of it can make them want to be together. What justice cannot do, tolerance will not do. Tolerance can form temporary and useful combinations of men of diverse races and religions and even conflicting ideologies; but tolerance is merely controlled antagonism; it can combine men but it cannot unite men. The peace of a mutual peril—the breaking of a levee, a hurricane, a war—is not peace but merely an armistice between peoples who will return to hostilities when the ebbing peril gives the first opportunity.

If the integration of the races in the secular order is to be anything more than cold justice, tolerance, or a co-operation compelled by mutual danger, there must be in and among the people a spirit which transcends ethnic differences, which is beyond likes and dislikes, and which resolves the conflicts of racial interest. In the fact that men have one Father, one Creator, in the fact that He has created all of them out of one substance and made them blood brothers, in the fact that all racial divisions of men have been equally endowed with capacities for self-fulfillment and have been given identical properties of mind and body, in the fact of their biological and psychic sameness there are manifest imperatives for good will among all men. Wherever men lift from these facts their moral and spiritual implications, they must move toward one another not as aliens who have no ground for peace and harmony but as men who, sharing a common and closely related life, find some part of themselves in every other man.

Increasingly in the secular society there are developing those social settings where the races meet amicably and in which the animal oneness can be lifted toward the level of human community. It has been demonstrated that where the members of various racial, cultural, and economic segments of society meet in the arts, sports, in a common patriotism, in municipal projects and programs, in the exercise of mutual citizenship, in civic services, labor unions, the armed services, there the leveling and binding quality of secondary and temporary interests, duties, and loyalties provides the time, the mood, the climate for the recognition and the practice of that broader and more basic bond which all people have as members of one human family. Such mutual activities are, so to speak, the temporary form over which the permanent arch may be built; when the arch is firm the form which gave it support may be safely removed. In time the form might deteriorate and collapse, but the arch becomes permanent. There are white Southerners whose racial prejudice will never be quite the same again; they have served with Negroes in the armed forces, competed with them and against them in college and professional sports, worked with them in municipal interests common to both. Over such forms the self-supporting arch of brotherhood has opportunity to set and to become enduring.

To speak of the brotherhood of man in the secular sense of the phrase may in the Christian view leave much to be desired; but it need not be, as it so often is, an appeal to a maudlin and hollow sentimentality which knows not the depth of the rift between man and man and which therefore withers under the first rebuff. It can be a fruitful appeal to the ancient and lean but tireless fact that from the beginning man was made one. The racially divided secular society can claim for its healing nothing more than this; the Christian ethic must offer nothing less.

9.

To All Men

Homo sum: humani nihil a me alienum puto.

—TERENCE

There is a duty which the Christian owes to all men irrespective of their conditions of race, culture, class, health, or creed. This is the area of human relationship referred to by the Apostle when he wrote to the Galatians, ". . . let us do good to all men. . . ."[1] This, then, is the endemic duty which all Christians owe to all men, a duty distinct from and in addition to that elemental duty which all men owe to all men. It is distinct and additional for two reasons: the understanding and appreciation of the nature of man which the Christian has in the Judeo-Christian tradition and the Christian's awareness of what he himself is in Christ.

The full force of the Christian rebuke of racial antagonism in all of its forms comes into focus and into effect, not in its concern for the Negro as Negro, but in its concern for the Negro as man. So long as we deal with the Negro as Negro, we skirt the central issue of his dignity and right as man. That the Negro is a man with

[1] Gal. 6:10b.

168

all the attributes of that classification few in our generation would deny; that he is dealt with according to the implications of that classification few would claim. What does the Christian owe to man as man? When we have answered that question we shall know automatically what the Christian owes to that man who has the subtitle Negro. We must therefore consider those Christian views of man which are especially pertinent to the problems of racial conflict.

The Christian doctrine of man involves many concepts which are only indirectly related to the problems of racial friction; however, within the Christian doctrine of man there are insights which thrust themselves upon us as especially applicable to the problems of ethnic antagonisms. Our purpose, then, is not to attempt a rounded and complete theological definition of the nature of man, but rather to state those Christian views of man which bear particularly upon the right of the Negro as a man to have, to belong, and to be, presenting these views in forms which indicate that morality which should be the special practice of the white Christian in his relationships to all Negroes.

If we are asked why all human life should be treated with respect, we are reduced in our answer either to an axiomatic or to a Biblical claim that every man has within him and as an essential and indestructible part of his being a native dignity. It is common among Jews and Christians to refer to this essential dignity of man, the worth and sacredness of his personality, in the Biblical term *the image of God*. This, of course, is a phrase which is so prolific— indeed, so prolific in its many contradictory definitions—that we cannot here even begin to describe its descendant ideas. But we are fortunate in the fact that we need only two suggestions from this fruitful expression, the first of which is that the proper study of the essential worth of man is not man but God, his Creator.

Much effort has been spent in trying to find within man some attribute or some group of peculiarities which would validate man's otherwise arrogant claim that he is significantly distinct from and infinitely superior to all other creatures in the world; and each of these discovered distinctions has in its turn been cited as "the image of God" in man. But we see the worth of the naked and irreducible man by looking, not at him, but at his Creator. Man's dignity is conferred upon him; his worth is bestowed. His value is the value of an autograph: the paper itself is of little value but the signature makes it precious. Man is unique among God's creatures not because he is a reasoning, toolmaking, cooking, or laughing animal, in these particulars distinct, but because God made him a special and preferred creature.

"Creatures," said Meister Eckhart, "are pure nothing." This is too strong for most of us even as hyperbole; but we must conclude at least that, whatever the creature is, his attributes are the works, not of him, but of his Creator. One of Eckhart's favorite verses of scripture reads: "All things were made through him, and without him was not anything made that was made."[2] Moreover, if we find the fundamental value of man, his essential dignity, within man, then we establish a condition of varying values and dignities among men, a prorated evaluation of men which contends that the essential and irreducible value of some is greater than the fundamental merit of others. This is the substructure for aristocratic and tyrannous societies rather than for democratic and Christian communities. The innate dignity to which the Christian faith refers in the phrase *the image of God* is universally shared in equal portions by all men, whatever all other circumstances may be.

The Christian view of man knows no graded scale of essential and fundamental worth; there is no divine right of whites which differs from the divine right of Negroes. Man's sacred uniqueness as a creature is not found in those productive powers which lead to cultural and material achievements; that would mean degrees of sacredness among human personalities. His value as a man is not lodged in his self-awareness, his ability to say "I am I"; that would mean that the saint and the mystic would be more valuable in the sight of God than the dullard and the brute. He is not of infinite worth because he alone in the animal kingdom has a ra-

2 John 1:3.

tional capacity; if so, the moron and the idiot would have to be declared essentially worthless by both God and man. His dignity as a creature has not to do with his ability to know right from wrong; if so, the pathological liar would be beyond the love of God. That these attributes are all essential to the nature of the complete man and must not be belittled is granted, but the accent upon the fact that man is so made is dangerous unless it be followed by the heavier stress upon the fact of man's Maker.

The Christian religion avoids this error, disclaiming entirely any grading of the essential worth of man. God made man and not some individual men or groups of men in His own image. By the phrase *the image of God* we are speaking, then, of what God has made, of that into which He breathed the breath of life, to which He gave the unique relationship of child as well as creature to Himself, to which He gave dominion over all earthly creatures, and upon which He bestowed all those distinctions which lift man into a super-animal realm. The glory of "the image of God" is in God and only reflectively in the image. The sacredness of man has to do with what man is only secondarily; it has to do primarily with the fact that God has made him, breathed into him a part of His own being, lifted him, taught him to walk, chastised and forgiven him, loved him, sought him, and in the final gracious act suffered for him on a cross. Apart from faith in such a God all talk of human dignity and equality is ultimately unsupportable.

This means that we cannot acclaim the sacredness of any man until we acknowledge the sacredness of all men; for the dignity and the holiness are not in man the created except as they are in God the Creator. Cancel that innate worth of man anywhere and it is canceled everywhere; deny it to one and it is denied to all. It is a glory which is in God and belongs to all men, or it is not in God and does not belong to any man. We do not begin to comprehend the meaning of the phrase *the image of God,* we have no inkling of the Biblical view of man, until we can look at the derelict, the profligate, the prodigal as well as at the saint and can know that there, however torn and faded it may seem, we are looking at the image of the Eternal. For the Christian, therefore, the sacredness, the infinite worth, of individual personality has nothing to do with culture or intellect or color or race or morality or faith; but it has to do with God, with the God who in His will and wisdom created all men in His image and destined them for His likeness.

Consequently, in the Christian view no human life is worthless; every human being has upon it the indelible and dignifying stamp of its Creator. The fact that it is a human life, that fact alone, qualifies it to share equally in that elemental worth which belongs to all men. However worthless the particular life may appear by the standards of men, it has nevertheless an irrevocable value; to assault that value in any man, to deface or ignore it, is not merely to repudiate that man but also to offend his Creator. The belief that every life, however repugnant on its surface, has its concealed value, its dignity, its right, that it must be reverently approached and dealt with—such a belief we assume to be the underlying principle of jurisprudence; we trust that it is elemental to the practice of medicine; but we are yet to make it the governing rule of human behavior in the relationship of the Christian to the Negro.

The Negro, no more and no less than the white man, has from God a conferred worth which men may deface and which he himself may deny but which no man can take away from him. He, too, is "the image of God" and, whether he accept it or not, one for whom Christ died. To say this is not to state an abstract sentimentality which can be kept ineffective in its isolation from the hard realities of life; on the contrary it is to establish that ground upon which the Negro with all other men can make his claim for the right to have, to belong, and to be. It is from this platform, from the stand of his innate dignity as a creature of God, that the Negro can move confidently, justifiably, and courageously into the arenas of society, law, economy, and industry with the powerful demand that his essential manhood be honored; and it is here that the white man must meet the Negro without advantage. This is not the least but the greatest common denominator equating

Negro and white. If racial justice begins anywhere else, it must end here or be a partial justice; if it begins here, in the knowledge of a sacred and shared value in a common Creator, it will spread like the vigorous kudzu over all the ranges of human relationship. It was in knowledge of this essential, irrevocable human dignity, sometimes inwardly divined but more often learned under Christian tutelage, that the Negro made his first abortive and later effective protests against the oppressions of a master-slave society, and from this footing he must now defend his gains and make all future claims. On this ground, a position from which he cannot be dislodged, he makes his stand: "I am a man; nothing human must be alienated from me."

From the rich phrase *the image of God* we draw also the conclusion that essential man has an innate dignity which must be respected, not only because he is a creature especially made and ordained by God, but also because he is a creature whom God loves. The fact that God loves man is so elemental and central to the Christian religion that we need not discuss it unless we intend to dissect the whole Christian faith. But we do need to stress the fact that the love of God confers the highest dignity upon man and indicates that ethic which should exist between the Christian and all men. By the elevating and dignifying grace of God man has in himself that toward which the love of God moves even in the giving of Himself. Hence every man is correct in his supposition that he—and, since the love of God is gracious and without prejudice, all other men—has in his basic nature that which is of infinite value in the sight of God. In this and in nothing else—in the creative love of God—do we find the signal honor that belongs to all men.

How do we Christians escape the fact that this truth has its ethical implications? Ludwig Feuerbach said that " 'God loves man' . . . in plain speech means, the highest is the love of man."[3] Such a statement may appear overly anthropocentric; but it is an

[3] Ludwig Feuerbach, *The Essence of Christianity,* Harper & Brothers, Torch-books, New York, 1957, p. 58.

ethical imperative which Christians can escape by defiance but not by denial. Feuerbach quotes Luther to say:

He who can truly conceive such a thing (namely, the incarnation of God) in his heart, should, for the sake of the flesh and blood which sits at the right hand of God, bear love to all flesh and blood here upon the earth, and never more be able to be angry with any man. The gentle manhood of Christ our God should at a glance fill all hearts with joy, so that never more could an angry, unfriendly thought come therein —yea, every man ought, out of great joy, to be tender to his fellow-man for the sake of that our flesh and blood. . . . This ought to be a furnace that should melt us all into one heart, and should create such a fervour in us men that we should heartily love each other.

And Feuerbach concludes, "How can the worth of man be more strongly expressed than when God, for man's sake, becomes a man, when man is the end, the object of the divine love?"[4]

When we have said that the Negro is a man, we have said that he is "the image of God" in that he is a creature especially made and wonderfully endowed by his Creator. But we have said also that he is one whom God loves and upon whom, therefore, the highest honor has been conferred. His value in the sight of God is the value of the sacrifice of Christ. God is no respecter of persons; the value He sets upon any man is the value He confers upon all men; His love is indiscriminate. And this complete and indiscriminate love which God has for all men and for the Negro as a man, this divine and universal love which by some men is spurned as a noxious fable, is the solid bedrock upon which the Negro must erect all his claims. If he forgets or lets the white man forget what he is in his essential being, he loses that footing on which he may wrestle successfully for social, economic, and legal justice and that leverage by which he is lifted to his full stature in all community settings. The Magna Charta of the Negro is the declaration: "I am a man whom God made and loves; nothing God intends for man must be denied to me."

Secondly, in the Christian view of man not only is every man

4 *Ibid.,* p. 57.

"the image of God" but, also, every man is archetypal; that is, every man has individuality. He is not a copy turned from a common matrix. Every man, however much he may resemble the color and physical configurations of his race or blend into the commonalities of humanity, is nevertheless newly created by an original act of God. Man, so to speak, is a handmade product upon whom the molding hands of his Maker have in each case left some distinguishing marks of His touch. God is not only the Maker of man; He is also the Maker of each man; and this Maker, contemptuous of sameness, permits no reprints. Each of His products is an original. In this fact, as Berdyaev would put it, in the "unrepeatability"[5] of personality, we have both the mystery and the grandeur, the peril and the sacredness of man. Herein is implied the particular worth which God has set upon each of his individual children. When a lamb is lost from the fold of the God who is shepherd, He does not content Himself in the thought that He has ninety-nine more, nor does He claim compensation for the loss of stock and buy a replacement; He must seek and save that which is lost. Before God no man can take the place of another or substitute himself for the value that is missing. By the word *individuality,* therefore, we mean the essential distinctiveness of every man. He is himself and not someone else. We mean not only that he is "a physical organism which maintains its discrete existence and has its peculiar and dated history"[6] but also that every man is spiritually unique. All men are to some extent alike; every man is to some extent a novelty.

All stereotyping of the Negro—that which is merely nominal and that which involves discrimination and segregation—falls before the simple fact that each Negro is a singular, inimitable, and irreplaceable product of the creative will and love of God. All Negroes have the essential dignity of man; each Negro is an in-

[5] Nicolas Berdyaev, *Slavery and Freedom,* Charles Scribner's Sons, New York, 1944, Part I.

[6] Reinhold Niebuhr, *The Nature and Destiny of Man,* Charles Scribner's Sons, New York, 1943, Vol. I, p. 54.

dividual instance of that dignity. Because of the essential uniqueness of every man you cannot look at one Negro and assume that you know all Negroes. You cannot learn all that there is to know about all Negroes save one and assume that this knowledge will somehow completely classify the remaining Negro. You cannot gather enough statistics for a safe prediction as to what a particular Negro will like or dislike, do or not do, have or not have, become or not become. All statistical data about anything other than the physical characteristics of man merely prove that one chart must be followed by another. The individual defies definition by data drawn from the masses; behind him is no precedent, about him no duplicate, before him no replacement. To know him you must know *him*. Such is the reply which the Negro has to statistics and clichés, and the absurdity of the white man's generalizations about the Negro—whether they are scientific or impulsive—is rebuked by the Negro's fundamental claim: "I am an individual and irreplaceable man whom God loves; deal with me on the basis of what *I* am."

The ethic which issues from this view of man requires that we recognize the singularity of every Negro, that he become alive to us as a sacred, unique, and irreplaceable individual, that we extract the man from the race, that we gain a vision of that man who has been submerged and obscured by color and race. We know that no age has so thoroughly collectivized and objectified human life as has the time in which we live. We have collectivized invention, charity, sports; we have reduced the yearnings and fears of people to charts and graphs; we have sorted and labeled men, putting them like so many graded potatoes into bins of religion, politics, social status, and race; and to this we have added the stereotyping of a whole race of people until the word *Negro* calls up not an individual person but a cliché, a classification. But the patient is not a case; the man who wields a "jackhammer" is not labor or a social security number; the victim of an automobile accident is not a holiday statistic; and the Negro is not a race, a caste, or a class. The Negro is not a commodity, or a political bloc, or a labor supply. He is not a category of crime, or illiteracy, or immorality; he is not a housing problem, or an educational problem, or any other kind of problem. The Negro is a man, with the foibles and frailities, the longings and fears, the hopes and hungers and aspirations of a man. He is an individual, unrepeatable, irreplaceable man who must be met and dealt with in his own right. Christianity has in the past made a major, if periodic, contribution to the recovery of the individual; it has in the present the titanic task of rescuing the individual once more from powers which are hostile to his individuality, beginning with that Negro whose face Christian people have helped to obscure.

Thirdly, in the Christian view of man, every man has the right not merely to an unhampered physical existence but also to personality. By the word *personality* we are describing in man "a metaphysical center deeper than all the qualities and essences which we can find and enumerate. . . ."[7] By the word *personality* we mean the self-conscious, self-transcendent, self-directing nucleus of human being; we mean that center of self, that "I-ness," that conscious subject or object of all external and internal experiences, which is referred to when a man speaks, thinks, or makes an assertion of self. The attributes of that essential self are many and varied, involving all the adjectives implied by "the image of God": self-awareness, rationality, wholeness, freedom, moral responsibility, decision, ambition, aspiration, as well as the opposites of some of these characteristics. The right to be a person or, in brief, the right to be, is fundamental in the Christian doctrine of man.

This right ends, of course, on that frontier of being which becomes the boundary of the other man's similar right. But, within this limitation, a man's right to be has its authority in that God who made him, loved him, and bestowed upon him his "unrepeatability." This is the prerogative of all men, even those who do not recognize the fact that their warranty for being is in the

---

[7] Jacques Maritain, *The Person and the Common Good*, Charles Scribner's Sons, New York, 1947, p. 29.

creative act of a loving God. Indeed, men do not need Christian doctrine to tell them so, but by a native impulse they have defied the first law of their physical nature with an instinctive sensing of the fact that preservation of the self is the first law of the spirit. We therefore get Kierkegaard's "defiant man who wills to be himself—apart from God"; we sense this will to be, sometimes bizarrely exhibited, often subtly intimated, in the most dissolute and revolting of literature's Sartrean characters; in life we see this will to be even in those infant little peoples who retreat for years before the annihilating pressures of the world but who suddenly and for no apparent reason turn and stand. When the assaults reach the last inner citadel of its being, even the craven soul will fight for its existence. This, then, the right to be a person, whether it show itself in hideous or beautiful form, is the *sine qua non* of human life.

To paraphrase Schweitzer, the Negro is the will to be in the midst of the will to be. His hunger for "selfness" is no less intense, no less varied than it is in other men. His hunger for personality may be deep, obscure, and devoid of self-consciousness; he may not understand what it is that throbs painfully in his breast under the insults that a white society pours upon his color and his race. Under such assaults he may writhe in violent retaliations or withdraw behind a curtain of feigned subserviency and forced laughter, preserving inviolate his inner castle. Or he may achieve, whether he become famous or not, a noble expression of the will to be. The gamut of possibilities runs through many variations, all of which are testimony to the fact that the will to be is of the essence of the Negro as man.

The hunger for being, whether pure or corrupt, is so deep in man, so native, so essential to his nature that we must see it as originally implanted in man by the creative will of God. It was not merely life that God breathed into man, not merely physical existence; even more, God imparted to man the will to be, the hunger for personality. Therefore, from the Christian point of view nothing could be more diabolical than a deliberate attempt

to destroy in any man his will to be a man or to deny him that
right, putting him under such physical or mental or emotional
harassments as would blow out this light within his brain and
cool the fever for being within his heart. Yet much of our racial
behavior, as we have seen, comes under this indictment. We want
the Negro as a body; as a physique he is a convenience. It is
therefore not too difficult to convince most men of the right of
the Negro to have. But we do not want the Negro as a personality;
as a person the Negro restricts, challenges, embarrasses, and defies
the uses to which we would put his body. What he is as a personality, when we recognize him as a person, rebukes our use of
him as an "animated tool." Therefore, we may let him have; after
a time and after a fashion we may let him belong; but the last
thing we want to do is to let him be.

"Man," said Erich Fromm, "is not a thing."[8] The Negro is a
man and is therefore not a thing. He must be dealt with, not as
an instrumentality, but as a person sacred in himself. To do otherwise is to desecrate what he is and simultaneously to destroy a
vital part of what we ourselves are. To use another person for the
fulfillment of oneself is to desecrate his essential personality and
is at the same time to destroy personality in ourselves. The assumption that we can use the Negro as a means to the white man's
end, that we can steal the energies of his spirit and concentrate
them in ourselves, an assumption which underlies many of our
race relations, is nothing more than a sophisticated sorcery, a civ-
ilized voodooism. We can draw power from the life of another
person only when we touch the hem of his garment in reverence
for his personality. So long as the Negro is to us a means to any
kind of end whatsoever and is not to us an end in himself, so
long as we see him as anything other than an expression of that
unique and irreplaceable personality with which God endowed
all men, we have abused the image of God in him and consequently and proportionately lost it in ourselves. The word *conse-*

[8] Erich Fromm, "Man Is Not a Thing," *Saturday Review*, March 16, 1957,
p. 9.

quently is a *non sequitur* to the world; to the world it does not follow that he who debases the image of God in any other person desecrates it in himself. And this is evidence that what goes out of a man when he abuses the personality of a fellow man departs so quietly, so largely unobserved, that he does not know what it is he has lost. His brother is dead, that he knows; but that he, too, has died a little in his brother's death he does not know. We are saying that to destroy the sacred and irreplaceable self of any person is, in the Christian analysis, to do mortal injury to that same quality in ourselves. The ego which does not find its alter ego in every other human being loses a part of itself; and the white man who does not find his own self in the Negro has abdicated an essential part of his own humanity.

For example, in the expression of vicious and passionate racial prejudice the white man allows the beast hidden in his soul to emerge and command. Newspaper pictures of the jeering, spitting, stone-throwing white crowds which have resisted the desegregation of public schools are sufficient evidence of this fact. And, in the atmosphere of unconscious stereotyping, where the status and the integrity of the Negro are gradually and even gently obscured, what happens is that the white man becomes in regard to the Negro an amoral creature, even though, and perhaps because, the Negro in such situations placidly accepts what the white man is doing to him. The white man by making something human alien to himself becomes the less human. He grows callous to the pains and hungers, the wounded spirits, the assaulted dignities, the tender longings of a fellow human being. That nerve which should ache when any human being is subjected to indignity has in him been completely anesthetized so far as the Negro is concerned. The tragedy of the white man is that he does not know what he is doing to himself and his Negro neighbor by his thoughtless, habitual conformity to the conventional patterns of a seemingly moderate but actually vicious discrimination. And the fact that he does not know is the measure of the destructive effect of his customs upon his own soul. For the first tragedy of many

white people in their relationship to the Negro—their tragedy
as well as the Negro's—is not that they are passionately alive
toward the Negro in hatred or in contempt but that they are dead
toward him in all understanding, identity of feeling, and simple
compassion. And the significant point for the white man is that
this is a death which is in him and not in the Negro. Unwilling
to let the Negro be, he ceases to be himself.

The Christian view of man, moreover, holds that a man has not
only the right to be himself but also the right to fulfill himself,
to be not only what he is at the moment but also all that he can
be through the unfolding of his potentialities. The full glory of
anything is the fulfillment of its potentiality; the Negro as a man
has the right to that glory. It was here, probably more than anywhere else, that Booker T. Washington defaulted his responsibility to his people. His clarion called Negroes to establish themselves agriculturally, economically, and industrially, abjuring the
poetic, artistic, and intellectual yearnings which stirred in their
hearts. They were, by his guidance, to be a practical, prudent, and
industrious people, leaving the fine arts to the whites who had
nothing better to do. He believed that the Negro could improve
his lot by making himself indispensable to the white man's social
order. His stratagem, if it had prevailed for long, would have
stifled many of that "talented tenth" who were to lift their race
by the full development and expression of their native talents.
From this fate the Negro was saved by the school of Miller, Du-
Bois, Johnson, which was to show that the writer's pen, the artist's
brush, and the surgeon's scalpel are as natural in the hands of the
Negro as are the pick and the hoe.

The Negro at his best has assumed that the nurture and the
expression of his fullest personality is not only the privilege of the
Negro but also his duty. He has assumed that "the souls of black
folk" contain all the mysteries and wonders, the heights and
depths, that are found in the souls of any people and that it is
their right and duty to bring out of their treasury whatever rich-
ness God has deposited. The Negro has believed himself to be

something more than manual dexterity and physical endurance. He has believed that the cultural lag of his people in the days before "the middle passage" can be dispassionately explained and that the explanations do not prohibit his entering into the cultural achievements of this day on equal footing with any other people. He has said with Kelly Miller, "Do you think that when the candle of genius has been lighted by fire from above it can be hid under a bushel of racial exclusiveness? Nay; rather, it is set on a candlestick and gives light unto all who grope in darkness. The Negro enters into the inheritance of all the ages on equal terms with the rest, and who can say that he will not contribute his quota of genius to enrich the blood of the world?"[9] He has said with James Weldon Johnson, "The pledge to myself which I have endeavoured to keep through the greater part of my life is: I will not allow one prejudiced person or one million or one hundred million to blight my life. I will not let prejudice or any of its attendant humiliations and injustices bear me down to spiritual defeat. My inner life is mine, and I shall defend and maintain its integrity against all powers of hell."[10]

In such yearnings for self-fulfillment we see all that is implied but also something more than what is meant when sociology speaks of self-realization. What is here claimed is not merely job opportunity, housing privilege, political status, or the freedom to use all one's native talents in chosen professions and avocations but, even more, the right of the essential self, the right of the soul to be itself and to become under the grace of God what it can be. There is a fullness which no material or social achievement can provide and for which sociology has no language equivalent to religious description. Beyond the rights of the civic person, beyond the rights of the social person, beyond the rights of the person as a physical being, there are the rights of the person

[9] Kelly Miller, *Race Adjustment*, The Neale Publishing Company, New York, 1910, pp. 44–45.
[10] James Weldon Johnson, *Negro Americans, What Now?* The Viking Press, New York, 1934, p. 103.

as person. The rights of the person qua person, beyond all physical, social, and civic modifications, include the yearning to be in its broadest but also its highest reaches: the desire for spiritual fulfillment. The right of the person as such means the right to pursue that fulfillment of self here and now in things physical and social but also in those ranges of the soul which are beyond the cramped quarters of time and space.

Such aspirations are, of course, as scarce among Negroes as they are among white people or any other racial groupings; but the evidence of such yearnings in the heart of one Negro is sufficient to show that the will to fulfill oneself occurs among all peoples. Whenever it occurs, it is the hallmark of man in full stature and its discouragement is a crime perpetrated not only against the individual in whom it occurs but also against the whole human family; for the advancement of mankind is made possible only when we permit and encourage all men to fulfill their lives at the level of their complete and exceptional possibility. Where society stunts the growth of any man, it deprives itself; if the contributions which the Negro has made to American culture through the arts, the sciences, the humanities, and the spiritualities were eliminated we should all be infinitely poorer. On the other hand, where some Negro, with or without our help, rises above the common level, we are all the better for it. It is, therefore, nothing short of stupidity for the white man, especially the Christian, to put impediments in the way of any Negro's progress toward his fullest personality.

The Christian ethic requires, however, not only that the white Christian permit but also that he foster the Negro's fullest personal development. The white Christian as a disciple of Christ must encourage and help the Negro regain his identity as a child of God, with all the honors, rights, and dignities appertaining to that title. Christians have the duty to encourage in all men a mature acceptance of themselves and of their right to be and of restoring to them their lost or sickened desire for fullness of personality. Every Negro who goes through this life ignorant of what he is and blind to what he could be is doubly the responsibility of the white Christian; for it was white Christians who helped to make him "dead to rapture and despair"; and it is Christians who have that Gospel which is dedicated to the principle of making dead men live and giving them a life more abundant.

Several years ago I revisited in my native state an artesian well which had been a boyhood haunt. As I got out of my car, I was met by an elderly Negro of the old school, who, holding his hat crumpled in his hand, shuffled toward me, saying, "Cap'n, can I have a little tobacco?" My reply was impulsive and instantaneous; but, as I review it now, I am sure that in its background was that New Testament scene in which Cornelius bows at the feet of Peter and Peter says to him, "Stand up; I myself also am a man."[11] So to this aged Negro, a personification of Uncle Tom, I said without thought, "If you want tobacco, put your hat on your head and don't call me 'Cap'n.'" Surely a part of the attitude of white Christian people and the service of the white Christian church toward the Negro must be founded on the spirit of this text: "Stand up; I myself also am a man."

But we must recognize that this is the easy part of the Christian duty toward the Negro in his recovery of personality. It is one thing to grant favors to a fawning Uncle Tom; it is quite another thing to give recognition to his son, with "a college diploma in his knapsack." It is one thing to rebuke the groveling manner and graciously proffer toward the humiliated Negro a helping hand; it is quite another thing to honor and encourage that self-reliant Negro who asks no favors and demands that we stand no longer between what he is and what he can be. It is one thing to give to another man his lost awareness that he, too, is the image of God, but it is quite different when he moves first and asserts what we have failed to give. The white Christian, watching a Negro rise to his full stature as a man, taking his rights, going where he belongs, and being what he is, without so much as a "by

11 Acts 10:26b (King James Version).

your leave" to the white man, can be inwardly stung with a galling sense of resentment, a resentment which can be traced to a deep, perhaps unconscious sense of guilt.

If to some extent it is true that white Christians are still dealing with a simple and humiliated people whose rise toward maturity we can self-contentedly credit to our generosity, to a larger and to an increasing extent we are confronted by a people who will spurn our self-flattering benevolences, seeing in them a subtle but very real debasement of their personality, and who will accept our help, if they need it, only if it be qualified by respect for their manhood. The Negro has come to that day when the white man's charity costs too much; and the white man has come to that day when he can no longer use the Negro as a means by which to practice his daily good deed. The question for white Christians is whether they can now rise to the occasion and achieve for their own sakes as well as his that respect for the Negro which will let him be what he is: an individual, personal man whom God created and whom God loves.

Christian love, if genuine, is never parochial; it does not halt at boundaries set by membership in "the household of faith." Indeed, the valor and the uniqueness of Christian love are not evident until it express itself where reciprocity cannot be expected. Christians are under command to do good to all men. The fact that a particular Negro is not a Christian or that he does not meet the white man's definition of a Christian in no way relieves the white Christian of his obligation to exercise a complete Christian charity toward that Negro. The Christian ethic begins not "out there" in the other person but "in here" in the new creature that one has become through Christ. The bases for human relationships are set for the Christian, not by conditions which pertain to the other person—his low estate, his disease, his class, his color, his virtue or vice, his worthiness or unworthiness—but by the radical quality of the Christian life. Christ, not the other person, determines the Christian's attitude and behavior.

The Christian, in other words, is never permitted to say, "Whatever my duty to others, I shall deal with this one as though he were not a man and as though I were not a Christian." Everything else varies; but the constant determining the ethical relationships of the Christian is his new being in Christ Jesus. His good will may or may not be merited by the other man; it may or may not be profitable to the other man; it may or may not be returned by the other man; but the imperative of his life is not from these but from Christ. What he sees "out there" in the other person may tempt his pity or his contempt, his hatred or his love; but what he is "in here" authorizes that his conduct toward the other person be Christian. His ethic, to use the common expression, is a vertical commitment which none of the fluctuating, horizontal conditions can alter. To such a man, color or the curl of the hair, culture or the lack of it, literacy or ignorance, health or disease, morality or immorality are superficial and irrelevant distinctions which have no bearing upon the intensity or the range of the Christian's good will. These have all been spanned by that spirit which, possessing the vital center of his being, brings all men within the orbit of his Christian love.

10.

Especially... the Household of Faith

I do not pray for these only, but also
for those who are to believe in me through
their word, that they may all be one;
even as thou, Father, art in me,
and I in thee, that they also may be
in us, so that the world may believe
that thou hast sent me.

—JOHN 17:20–21

We have climbed, thus far, from a vast plain on which we considered what all men owe to all men by virtue of their common manhood to a plateau on which we viewed the duty of the Christian to all men because of what he is and because of what they are. Now our ascent takes us to those highlands where we consider what the Christian owes to the Christian. The Christian view of human unity, we have said, holds that there is for Christians a spirit of cohesion for which the world at large is not ready, a union which is ultimate and indivisible, a bond beyond and stronger than the slender and elastic ties of physical kinship and even beyond all the spiritual implications of that kinship. This is the area of human relationship to which the Apostle referred when he wrote, ". . . especially to those who are of the household of faith."

This is not to suggest that Christians merit a better treatment than other men; it is not to suggest that Christianity is a clannish fellowship in which the special charities of the faith are restricted to the members of the fellowship. But it is to say that between Christian and Christian there should flow lines of communication which do not exist where non-Christians are involved. The particularism which is suggested by the accent of this chapter excludes no one from the scope of Christian good will, but it does encourage a special affection between those who are members of the same faith.

I have stated already that Acts 17:26a is the Christian declaration to a racially divided secular world: "And he made from one every nation of men to live on all the face of the earth. . . ." I have stated, also, that it is wasteful to require of Christians nothing more than elemental decency and thus to discredit the quality and the reconciling power of that unity which Christians have in Christ. I have implied that this verse was by no means Paul's final, incisive, or summary word on the subject of human unity, but rather that it was an ingratiating statement of elemental physical kinship, by which Paul sought to establish a *rapprochement* between himself and his Athenian audience. For Christians to use this verse as the basis for harmonious relationships between the races within the Christian family is to take Paul at his least, is to ignore entirely the distinctive witness of the Christian ethic, and is to leave the unfortunate and fallacious impression that human nature, made aware of itself and its kind, can then and on its own solve the bitterest and most complex problems of human antagonism.

When the Apostle addressed himself to the subject of Christian unity, as he so frequently did, he nowhere said that human solidarity is a matter of physical identity or suggested that human conflicts can be resolved by an appeal to that fleshly oneness which all men share. Brotherhood was not to Paul a sequel to creature-hood; and, to him, the solution of human estrangement, a spiritual problem, was not to be found in man's animal nature. The clearest texts for Christian race relations within the Christian family are Pauline declarations, but the summary uses we have made of Acts 17:26 are not congenial to Pauline thought.

For Paul the ethnological problem within the Christian fellow-ship was dissolved, not in the awareness of man's biological iden-tity, but in that oneness which men have in Christ, not "after the flesh" but "after the spirit," not in the solid and shared flesh of men but in the broken and shared body of Christ, not in consan-guinity but in communion. Christians—Negroes and whites—are not merely members of one flesh but, even more, members of one "body." They have their oneness not by the common blood of their physical life; but, for them, those "who once were far off have been brought near in the blood of Christ."[1] If there is a Magna Charta of Christian human relations, it is not Acts 17:26 but Galatians 3:28 and duplicating passages in the writing of the Apostle: Ephesians 2:13–22, I Corinthians 12:4–27, Colossians 3:11. "There is neither Jew nor Greek, there is neither slave nor free, there is neither male nor female; for you are all one in Christ Jesus."[2]

This passage, like many others, is saturated with Paul's passion-ate confidence that enmities, divisions, and dissimilarities are abolished by that Christ who serves as our reconciliation and our peace and who in his flesh has conquered those hostilities which are native to all flesh. All varieties—even some which are norm-ally lauded: talents, intelligence, knowledge, race, culture, nation-ality—are consumed and obliterated by that spirit which makes all one. The oneness of Negro Christians and white Christians is not the animal oneness of a common flesh but "For by one

[1] Ephesians 2:13b.
[2] Galatians 3:28.

Spirit we are all baptized into one body—Jews or Greeks, slaves or free—and all were made to drink of one Spirit."[3] This is human unity at the core of being: we are one clay but into that clay has been breathed one breath of God, a breath restored in the Spirit of Christ.

Thus, to Paul, there is a catholicity of divine grace which immediately nullifies all distinctions between those who are embraced by it. Even Luther, who believed that "In the world and according to the flesh, there is great difference and inequality of persons; and the same must be diligently observed"[4] read in Galatians 3:28 a bond of Christian unity which cancels difference and inequality, saying: "Contrariwise, in Christ there is no law, no difference of persons, there is neither Jew nor Grecian, but all are one."[5]

The Jew is abolished. Paul not only writes of the Jew as the prototype of religious legalism but is also insisting that the Jew as the symbol of inherited ethnic distinction disappears in the embrace of Christ. Pride of ancestry—racial pride—permeated the Jewish cry, "We have Abraham as our father."[6] To the claim of John the Baptist that ". . . God is able from these stones to raise up children to Abraham"[7] Paul adds that in Christ He has indeed done so; within the fellowship of Christ ancestry loses all significance; it is no longer either badge or stigma; for by adoption all Christians are sons of Abraham: "And if you are Christ's, then you are Abraham's offspring, heirs according to promise."[8]

In the Christian fellowship there can be no "Jew," that is, no ethnic distinction; for, by implication, all racial dissimilarities are dismissed; therefore, the substituting of the word *Negro* for the word *Jew* in this text is both logical and, for our times, per-

[3] I Corinthians 12:13.
[4] Martin Luther, *A Commentary on Saint Paul's Epistle to the Galatians,* 1848 edition, p. 350.
[5] *Ibid.*
[6] Matthew 3:9.
[7] *Ibid.*
[8] Galatians 3:29.

190

tinent. The question as to whether or not a Negro should be admitted into the fellowship of other Christians should not even be debatable; if he applies as a Christian he does not apply as a Negro. To discuss his admission on the basis of his race is to raise an issue for which there is no room in the Christian conscience or in the Christian community. To raise the question is to give *ipso facto* evidence that the conscience and the community have both surrendered their right to the appellation *Christian*. This, of course, is to speak ideally about the matter.

Actually, however, the question in one form or another will thrust itself soon or late into every white congregation. It may come as a practical test in which the white church is taken completely by surprise when a Negro applies for membership. It may arise when denominational resolutions, pronouncements, home missions and social progress programs which deal with racial problems are pressed upon the local church. It may be put by the young people when they begin to wonder why the Christian church has to be the last segregated institution in American social life. It may be forced by those who are determined that the church remain exclusive and who want by official action of the local church to fix the *status quo*. It may break into the open when the sensitive and guilty conscience of the excluding church seeks to defend and justify its exclusion. It may speak for the awakening and maturing spirit of those Christians who begin to understand and accept the inclusiveness of the Body of Christ. In one way or another in every segregated white church the question will be put and the issue joined.

It is best that the question of Negro membership in formerly white churches be proposed against a background in which the meaning of and the qualification for church membership can be thoroughly explored, in which the scriptural and spiritual bases for the integration of Negro and white Christians in the same church can be soundly laid, and in which the mood of the white Christians is being prepared for a genuine and complete acceptance of their Negro fellows in Christ. Once the awesome, stunning question has been put to the white congregation in the abstract and in theoretical discussion, fear of the question itself will begin to diminish and opportunities for reasonable Christian discussion will be opened.

Moreover, the question should rise or should be logically drawn from the repositories of Christian concepts of faith, morals, and human unity and should appeal, not to secular notions of equality, but to that unity which Christians have in Christ. Where such an appeal is ineffective, the integration of Negro and white Christians in the same church will be forced, artificial, fragile, and dangerous. In such a situation the Negro member would again be humiliated and the Body of Christ ruptured. Where a concrete proposal for Negro membership in a white church is preceded by an educational and spiritual preparation of the white Christian, the possibilities for a harmonious integration of the two races in the same church are greatly strengthened.

The Greek is abolished. That is, social distinction is wholly irrelevant in the Christian fellowship. Knowledge, wealth, and culture are linked to ignorance, poverty, and simplicity by a love which levels all grades of distinction. In a line which makes this the plainer and which leaves no doubt about it, Paul, in writing to the Colossians, adds the word *Scythian,* declaring that the Scythian, "the barbarian's barbarian," loses all disgracing marks of class within "the household of faith." He contends, moreover, that Christ fuses in oneness the poles of greatest social diversity: "there is neither slave nor free." Cato, the virtuous guardian of Roman morals, advised farmers "to sell worn-out iron implements, old slaves, sick slaves, and other odds and ends that have no further use on the farm." But the Christian Apostle by his words invites all the odds and ends of humanity into full status in the Christian family.

In our day there is a strange and disturbing development, particularly among Protestant Christians. That rare Negro who is accepted as an equal in the white Protestant church must first qualify socially or professionally. He escapes the stigma of race only by achieving the standard of class; or, so to speak, he ceases to be the excluded "Jew" only by becoming the acceptable "Greek." It is required of the Negro applicant, not that he prove himself as a Christian, but primarily that he match in his life the cultural stratum which characterizes the particular church to which he applies. Thus the socially stratified Protestant church violates that catholicity which the Apostle required, even in the seemingly tolerant act of accepting a Negro into its membership.

Male and female are abolished. The superficial division of mankind into races, colors, physiognomies, nationalities, is as nothing compared with the division of all divisions into sexes—male and female. Perhaps Paul added this phrase *male and female* for emphasis as well as for its practical applications; for here is a radical, universal, cherished, and beneficial division of humanity which has its foundations deeper in nature than any other distinction; yet this difference, too, is abolished in Christ. Biologically, in the creation, God said, "Let there be male and female"; spiritually, in Christ, God said, "Let there be neither male nor female." So, in Bishop Lightfoot's phrase, "even the primeval distinction of male and female"[9] is consumed in that universal quality which Christ bestows upon all who are in him. Thus not only is the unifying power of Christ able to remove arbitrary and artificial distinctions between men, to break down all unnatural and fabricated walls, but it is also able to obliterate the imputations of those human differences which are natural and original. The physical fact remains; the divisive implications of that fact—all hints of superior and inferior status and all estranging dissimilarities—are extirpated by a Spirit which makes all one. Biologically, the Negro Christian does not cease to be a Negro nor does the white Christian cease to be a Caucasian; yet, in Christ, the racial differential is transcended and they are one. The ancient scoffer's description of Christianity as "sexless, homeless, nationless" is a figurative

[9] H. D. M. Spence (editor), *The Pulpit Commentary,* Funk and Wagnalls Company, London and New York, 1913, p. 146 of volume on Galatians and Ephesians.

yet precise description of what the Christian community should actually be.

However, in the Christian fellowship dissimilarity dissolves not in uniformity but in community. It is not required that the Greek become a Jew or that the Jew become a Greek. Paul recognized, indeed, that there are differences which do not destroy but serve the oneness of Christians: "Now there are varieties of gifts but the same spirit. . . ."[10] In the Christian fellowship each person retains the identity of his individual and irreplaceable personality, but all have relatedness, oneness, through that Christ whose power has worked its silent and invisible transformation in them. We "are one body in Christ, and *individually* members one of another."[11] Like assorted iron filings around a central magnet, each retaining its own shape and mass and to some degree its separateness but all related to each other, so Christians retain their personal identities but in Christ the divisive allegations of those diverse identities are canceled. Under his influence there is a molecular transformation which may be externally invisible but which nevertheless binds Christian to Christian.

Interracial harmony among Christians is not a question of pretending that there are no differences; in the world differences are apparent and differences are real and it is naïve and dangerous to pretend that they are not. But in the Christian community divisive differences remain only as a phantasm of deluded minds and prejudiced hearts. Where the Christian sees his fellow Christian as anything other than a Christian, he has called forth a specter which has its embodiment only in his own mind and heart, an apparition which fades and disappears as he himself is lost in Christ.

[10] I Corinthians 12:4a.
[11] Romans 12:5.

11.

Toward a Racially United Church

---

*To labour for a perfect redemption from
this spirit of oppression is the great
business of the whole family of
Christ Jesus in this world.*

—JOHN WOOLMAN

Not long ago a professor of political science,
returning to this country from England for one of his periodic
surveys of the American scene, questioned the depth and durabil-
ity of this country's current religious revival. There are, of course,
ample and solid grounds for such suspicions, and any appraisal
of the present American mood which ignores this religious phenomenon will be incomplete. But the criterion which the visitor
laid down as the ultimate test of the genuineness of the religious
revival is so arbitrary and fractional as to become unreliable. He
wrote, ". . . there is a practical test coming that will be, I think,
decisive. If five years from now, in those areas in which organized
religion is strongest—that is, the South—desegregation *in the
churches* is not pretty nearly complete, I shall take the liberty of

195

doubting the existence of a great spiritual upheaval."[1]

One is tempted to bring several rejoinders against this judgment; but of interest to us is the fact that this critique is characteristic of those which idealize the racial problem, ignoring the amoral and nonracial factors which help perpetuate a racially divided society. We have seen that the woodworms of prejudice and racial oppression, even when they disappear completely, leave behind a vermiculated social order, weakened and disfigured by the irregularities they have eaten into its structure. This hard sociological and historical fact must not be ignored when we consider the persistence of racial division in the church.

The tendency of social patterns to continue far beyond their original function is an ironic fact which has direct bearing upon the racial split in the church. We have confessed, as we must, the principal and primary role of racial prejudice in dividing the church; we have acknowledged also the judgment which this continuing separation holds against the moral and spiritual quality of white Christians; but if the days of division are to be shortened, we must be mindful of and direct some of our energies toward those "senseless agencies" which, apart from all strictly racial considerations, preserve the racially divided church. It will be our purpose in this concluding chapter to explore the nonracial and semi-racial factors intertwined with prejudice in dividing the church and to suggest how we may best meet and reduce the hidden and accidental allies of racial division in the Christian church.

We are approaching such a perplexingly complicated sociological phenomenon that we cannot view it all at once as though it were on flat canvas but must walk around it and study its several facets as a statue is studied. On the one side we see the racially separate and exclusive white Christian churches. By "separate" we mean that these churches are, as official religious bodies, established along racial lines. By long tradition, if not by official

---

[1] D. W. Brogan, "Unnoticed Changes in America," *Harper's Magazine*, February, 1957, p. 27 (italics his).

policy and pronouncement, they are built, supported, and governed by white communicants. The official denominational titles of such churches never use the restrictive modifier *white*, but such a restriction is nevertheless assumed by members of both races and is generally honored by Negroes either to avoid personal embarrassment or as a part of racial etiquette. By "exclusive" we mean that openly or covertly white Christian churches prohibit the admission of Negroes into church membership and discourage the attendance of Negroes at services of public worship. It is tacitly understood by Negroes and whites that "whosoever will may come," when these words appear on the board or bulletin of such a church, applies only to members of the white community. From this side the problem of the racially divided church suggests that it has a simple and easy solution: let the white Christians be Christian and welcome all races to their fold and the gap is closed and the Body of Christ healed of its wound.

Obviously a spirit of welcome or at least tolerance on the part of white Christians is prerequisite to any permanent solution of racial separation in the church. As long as the white Christian church remains racially exclusive or discriminates against those Negroes who are admitted, Negro churches must remain racially separate. But is racial snobbery, however adequate it may be, the only barrier between Negro and white Christians and their churches? If the walls of spiritual isolation between Negro and white Christians were immediately and completely demolished, would there not still remain between their churches much impassable debris which would have to be carted away? Specifically, are there not purely mechanical factors giving aid and comfort to those who want to keep the church racially divided? Are there not also in the nature of the American forms of Protestant churches laudable qualities which nevertheless have a perverse effect upon racial unity within the church? We must examine the white Christian church to discover what these nonracial but divisive factors are and to determine how their hindrance of racial unity may be relaxed.

But if the white church is on one side of the problem of separation, the Negro church is on the other. It is, as we have seen, a historical fact that the white man made and keeps the Negro church a necessity of wholesome Negro life. If we were viewing the existence of the Negro church for the purpose of moral judgment, the onus of that judgment would, of course, be upon the white man. But, wherever we place the blame for its existence, the Negro church is a fact, and that fact in itself prolongs the racial division of Protestant Christianity. It is well, therefore, to ask in what sense the Negro church is a contributory factor in perpetuating the racial cleavage in the church.

Negro churches do exist; as religious bodies they are both inclusive and separate. They are inclusive in the sense that white applicants for membership are accepted and white communicants are warmly, even deferentially, welcomed at services of public worship. But Negro churches are nevertheless separate; that is, like white churches, they are built, supported, and governed by a racially constant constituency. In some cases, indeed, the official denominational titles of such churches carry adjectives which indicate their racial character. We are confronted by an interesting anomaly: we have white Christian churches which in official policy and pronouncement are interracial but in spirit and in practice are exclusive; we have Negro Christian churches which in title, purpose, and policy are officially racial but in spirit and practice are inclusive. We must therefore examine the Negro church, putting to it questions similar to those we address to the white church, if we are to know all the nonracial and semi-racial factors which sustain the division in the church.

We are assuming, as we put these questions, that separate churches, although not so vicious as segregating churches, nevertheless do and will continue to cast a racial stigma. A denomination which is divided from a sister denomination only by racial identity, however freely a few venturesome members may move from the one side to the other, provides a setting for the renewal of prejudice and discrimination between the races. The Negro church, however many its merits and services to its people, is a symbol of the white man's racial pride, discrimination, and exclusiveness; until the separate Negro church disappears—which means a simultaneous disappearance of the separate and exclusive white church—the conflict between white and Negro Christians cannot be considered resolved. This conclusion the religious leadership among Negroes either does not share or is reluctant to declare. In fact, agitation for integration in the churches has thus far come, not from Negro churchmen, but primarily from a few white church leaders. The maximum request made by one hundred Negro churchmen some years ago was not that the churches be racially one but rather that the white Christian churches "present the open door" to Negroes. We shall ask, shortly, why their suggested program is so modest. Meanwhile it is here held that it is not enough for the white churches to present the open door to Negroes, reciprocating the courtesy which Negro churches extend to whites. If the church is to be the church of Christ all racial designations must go.

Divisive Factors Common to White and Negro Churches

First, let us place on the record those extra-racial yet divisive factors common to both white and Negro churches. The merging of racially dissimilar churches, even where race is the only dissimilarity, is seriously hampered by the same impediments which prevent the merging of churches and denominations that are racially identical. Indeed, if by some miracle the racial tensions between whites and Negroes were immediately and completely erased, the years of grace granted by our visiting political scientist would scarcely suffice for the removal of those purely mechanical and ecclesiastical barriers now separating Negro and white churches. For what we are saying is that those same historical, social, psychological, and mechanical factors which perpetuate the denominational divisions of white Protestantism apply, with minor exceptions, to the racially divided denominations and, apart from racial considerations, serve as wedges between Negro and white churches. Among the divisive forces common to both churches are the following: denominational tradition, sentiment, and pride; the fear of lost identity; administrative complexities; the inherent urge of established organizations to expand, to continue, and to solidify; the vested interests and ambitions of individuals involved in the ecclesiastical structure; the constraint which specified legacies exercise upon present and future church activities; contrasts in types and moods of worship.

In the main these factors operate in both directions: from the younger and weaker Negro denominations as well as from the older and stronger white denominations. These common elements of division are compounded by one set of modifiers in the white churches and by another and different set of modifiers in the Negro churches; but it will be found that one racial section of the church is little more fluid and amenable to proposals for merger than is the other. Thus there are two crevasses which must be safely bridged in the successful blending of Negro and white churches: the racial division and the ecclesiastical division. No one who appreciates the depth and breadth of the chasms to be crossed will expect an early success. Even where religious bodies are identical in race, doctrine, and polity and where union has been sincerely proposed and long studied, the merger hoped for never materializes or is approached with deliberate slowness. As regrettable as this fact may be, it is nevertheless true that the extra-racial elements of division are sufficient to keep Negro and white churches separate for many years. Certainly we cannot expect that an ecclesiastical cleavage which is further complicated by racial conflict will dissolve more rapidly than one which is not affected by racial tension.

Divisive Factors Peculiar to Negro Churches

We note, secondly, that there are amoral yet divisive factors which are peculiar to Negro churches, and we see these factors in the multiple character of the Negro church, the many and varied roles which it plays in Negro life. Negro churches were originally formed, not to discriminate against white Christians, but to provide a safe and congenial religious setting for those Negro Christians who were smarting under the racial slurs of their fellow Christians. This was certainly a sufficient and justifiable ground for the establishment of a separate church. But from this original beginning there have evolved two conditions which hamper the merging of Negro and white Christians in a racially indivisible church. These conditions must be examined if we are to understand the complexity of the problem and are to appreciate in patience the time which must be consumed in removing the racial line that divides so much of Protestant Christianity.

First, as has been mentioned elsewhere, the newly formed Negro churches quickly multiplied their functions in Negro life. To their original *raison d'être* there began to adhere almost immediately numerous lesser but significant and related purposes and roles. In a word, Negro churches soon became for their people the primary, indeed the sole, social unit. Churches were not merely churches, settings for the unrepressed worship of an otherwise oppressed people, a refuge and a strength; but, being that, the Negro churches became for their people much more than that. Here was family life in the broad sense where family life in the narrow sense was prohibited or restricted. Here were the cells in which protest and rebellion against oppression were engendered and first expressed. Here, ready made, were school and forum and social laboratory for the general masses of Negroes and for the special training of those Negroes who showed leadership capabilities. Here in their togetherness in the church Negroes found their strongest social leverage and felt those centripetal forces which gave them community in a world that would have them scattered and ineffective. It is impossible to exaggerate the role which the Negro church has played as the total "social cosmos" of Negro life.

In more recent years the Negro church has lost some of its

central and dominant influence over Negro life; it remains, however, despite the rivalry of the Negro press, the N.A.A.C.P., the family, and the club, as the most forceful and fruitful, the most influential and reliable social institution affecting the total life and development of the Negro. Much of the Negro leadership still has its beginning and at least its early rise within the church. Such secular organizations as the N.A.A.C.P. frequently hold their local meetings under the auspices of and within the church and sometimes in programs which are strikingly similar to religious services. The Negro still has in his church, therefore, a power for racial solidarity; a voice of protest and of hope; a training ground for his developing leadership; a leverage for political, economic, and social advancement—all of which are presently irreplaceable. It is entirely unlikely that he will in the near future exchange this potent social unit for the dubious honor of worshiping in a church controlled and dominated by the white man and in which he would lose at once those beneficial by-products which his own church, self-owned and self-controlled, has so liberally produced.

The Negro wants the privilege of worshiping in and belonging to any church of his choosing as a child of God, unhindered and unmolested by slight or slur reflecting upon his race. But it would be folly for him to purchase that privilege or to gamble for it at the expense of that institution which more than any other has procured his freedom and his rise toward the dignities of full manhood and citizenship—his own church. It should be obvious from the spirit of these words that this is not a white man's subtle plea for a continued separation of the races within the Body of Christ but is rather an attempt to face with honesty one of the seldom-mentioned factors which will continue to perpetuate the racially divided church and which rises from the Negro's side of the cleavage.

Second, the existence of the Negro church on the American scene as a separate and self-sufficient social unit gives the white man a rationalization for his own exclusiveness. The existence of the Negro church, in other words, supplies the missing arc over which the prejudice and exclusiveness of white Christians may run in complete and vicious circle. By his prejudice and his exclusiveness the white Christian made the Negro church a necessity of wholesome Negro life; by his continuing prejudice and exclusiveness the white Christian prevents the disappearance of the Negro church as a distinct social unit: the Negro cannot and will not surrender the racial character of his church so long as its original reason for being remains in effect. Since it is patent that the Negro Christian will not now receive in churches of a white majority those satisfactions of having, belonging, and being which are his religious experience in his own church, it is also evident that he has no option and must for some time maintain his racially separate church. To that separate church, however, white Christians can and do point as a justification for their own exclusiveness. Their words are familiar: "Don't they (the Negroes) have their own churches? Don't they prefer to be among their own?" And on this theme there are many variations, all of which shift the blame for the separated church from the white man to the Negro. Thus the circle is completed: the existence of the Negro church is necessitated by white exclusiveness; white exclusiveness justifies and entrenches itself in the fact that there is a separate Negro church.

Divisive Factors Peculiar to White Protestant Churches

It was suggested earlier that the white Protestant churches may contain in their American forms qualities which, though in themselves laudable, have a perverse effect upon racial unity in those churches. Let us now explore that possibility and set down those nonracial yet divisive factors which are peculiar to white Protestant churches. We look for these divisive factors, not in the area of the churches' faith, but in the area of the churches' order, meaning by the word *order* the organizational structure and function of the churches. The denominational divisions of the church arose primarily from theological disputes and national alignments; but the racial split in the church, though it may assume denominational lines, has no genesis in doctrinal disputes. There are no theological factors dividing Negro and white Christians. Moreover, the many Protestant denominations are almost unanimous in condemning the racial division of the church as a sinful disobedience of the will of Christ and as a tragic destruction of that unity which all Christians have in him. It is correct to say, therefore, that the declared faith of the churches is racially inclusive; but from the order of the churches, from their form and function, come those barriers which assist prejudice in keeping most white churches racially exclusive. These barriers have to do, then, with the polity of the churches and with the nature of the fellowship within those churches.

It will be found that the factors buttressing exclusiveness in the white Protestant churches are components of the Protestant concept of the nature of the church. They are related to principles which are basic to the American forms of Protestantism: the separation of church and state, the voluntariness of church membership, the democratic or representative character of church government, the social and familial functions of the church. In the Protestant view these are laudable, cherished, and indispensable attributes of the church. Since it is unlikely that the Protestant churches—white or Negro—will sacrifice these qualities, which they hold to be of the essence of Protestantism, in order to accommodate a program of racial unity, it is well to understand in what sense these qualities permit a racial split in the churches and how the exclusiveness which they allow can be avoided.

To explore those extra-racial factors which are peculiar to white Protestant churches requires that we set the free Protestant churches over against the state-related churches and the Roman Catholic church. We do so, not to make odious comparisons, but to stress the fact that racial unity faces obstacles within American Protestantism which it does not face within the Roman Catholic church or within Protestant state churches. To be sure, Protestants can reply that their churches, which strongly accent the familial and social functions of the church, offer potentialities for racial unity exceeding those available in other Christian communions, a unity that is not merely official and ceremonial but also genuine. They can argue that, whereas desegregation in state and Roman churches is merely desegregation, Christians of the various races can have in the intimate fellowship of Protestant church life an integration worthy of the name. This is a plausible contention; but it is hazardous to exhibit as an asset to racial unity a condition which is thus far an obvious liability. As long as the walls of segregation stand in the free white Protestant churches, the superior merits of the Protestant concept of Christian fellowship must remain hypothetical.

As we look more closely at those qualities which are of the essence of American Protestant church life but which permit or foster racial division in the churches, we find that they are three in number: the freedom of the churches from federal edict, the freedom of the churches from episcopal edict, and the familial and social function of the churches. The first is relatively unimportant and is mentioned primarily as a matter of record; the second is more significant, exposing us to the contrasting Protestant and Roman Catholic records of desegregation; and the third is the most important, uncovering a weakness inherent in the Protestant concept of Christian fellowship and giving further occasion for an analysis of the difference between Protestant and Roman Catholic ventures into the realm of racially integrated church life.

Let us glance first at the suggestion that a church free from federal edict is more susceptible to racial division than is a state-supported or state-controlled church. In *An American Dilemma* Gunnar Myrdal makes the surprising statement that state-supported churches are more democratic than are those which are free from such a relationship to the state and implies that in state-supported churches the problem of class and race distinction is eliminated. He says, "In one particular respect the great split into denominations and individual congregations in America is anti-democratic in its results. It makes for a greater manifestation of social class distinction than there would be if most people belonged to the state-supported church."[2] Certainly there is truth in the inference that the social stratification of Protestant churches is partially the result of the freedom of those churches and that such social stratification contributes to the racial division of the churches. Indeed, it would be interesting to determine—if there were any way to do so—whether the flight of Protestant churches to the suburbs of large towns and cities has been motivated by the desire of the communicants for uniformity of social identity, including racial similarity.

However, the implication that the racial divisions would automatically find oneness in churches state-supported and state-controlled is weak on two counts. In the first place, a church membership conferred upon all citizens at the time of their birth could give them the meagerest kind of desegregation within the church without removing those acts of discrimination and segregation which in this country prompted the Negro to find a less oppressive setting for his worship than that provided by the discriminative white church. We know from the American experience that a citizenship which is a native right of all the people does not guarantee to all of them freedom from discrimination and segregation within the state. We cannot assume that a church membership which is a concomitant of citizenship will guarantee to all members freedom from discrimination and segregation within the church.

Furthermore, the suggestion that racial segregation would be eliminated in the state-supported church presumes a state favorable to the integration of the races. Given a state which protects the rights of all its citizens, a church which is dependent upon that state can be expected to conform to the general democratic policies of that state. However, where the state itself is the champion

[2] Gunnar Myrdal, *An American Dilemma,* Harper & Brothers, New York, 1944, p. 868.

of segregation, the church which is dependent upon or closely related to that state will be tempted to conform to the antidemocratic policies of the state. The first condition may prevail in Sweden and in the Church of Sweden—the probable background of Gunnar Myrdal's tribute to the democracy of state-supported churches—but the second condition is found today in the Union of South Africa and the Dutch Reformed churches. Even though state and church are officially separated in South Africa, the role played by the Dutch Reformed churches in that country can be accurately cited as state-related in the strictest sense. And it is here, where state and church are in closest collaboration and where each is dependent upon the other, that church and state have fashioned the most thorough of all patterns of racial segregation within the state and within the church. If it is true that in the United States the separation of church and state has made possible the social stratification of the Protestant churches, it is also true that in South Africa church and state have in closest co-operation produced and sanctioned the most extreme forms of racial oppression.

On the one hand we must agree that the freedom enjoyed by American Protestant churches does provide opportunity for class and race distinction within the church. But on the other hand we cannot conclude that a close tie between church and state will necessarily guarantee to racial minorities their rightful place within the church. Such freedom permits division but it does not make division inevitable. Moreover, we cannot agree that Christian fellowship is merely a human relationship falling into that area of justice over which the state has jurisdiction and in which it can exercise coercive action. The racial alienation of Christian from Christian must be canceled within the church and by those spiritual powers to which the church can appeal or the problem of separateness will not be solved at all. The state can to some extent establish in the secular order the justice owed by all men to all men; but the love which Christians owe to Christians is entirely beyond that realm in which the state can exercise control over the affairs of men.

The second extra-racial factor which in white Protestant churches permits racial exclusiveness is the freedom of American Protestants from episcopal edict. This characteristic, again, is permissive of racial division rather than racially divisive. To see the picture clearly we must lay the Protestant failure beside the Roman Catholic success. It is a fact that there are still numerous Roman Catholic churches which are racially segregated, principally in the South; nevertheless, the pace of desegregation within the Roman Catholic church puts to shame the progress of desegregation within American Protestantism. By the most charitable definition the number of interracial Protestant churches in the United States is probably less than a thousand; against this paltry achievement we must set a Roman Catholic record commendable both in the number and in the percentage of its interracial churches. If we assume, as Protestants will, that Protestants are not in creed and conduct ethically inferior to Roman Catholics, then we must ask why there is this contrast in their records of desegregation within the church.

There are two principal answers to this question, one of them being that all Protestant churches in the United States are to some extent democratic or representative in their forms of government and that therefore none of them can exercise over their people the compulsory episcopal edicts which are available to the hierarchy of the Roman Catholic church. Whereas a Roman Catholic bishop can by his official word and despite the opposition of laymen desegregate a parochial school, hospital, or church, the loftiest declarations of official Protestant bodies have only a counseling and persuasive effect upon the local churches.

It is self-evident that Protestants cannot exchange the benefits of their freedom for the efficiencies of ecclesiastical autocracy, even when that autocracy is beneficent, without ceasing to be Protestant. It is equally obvious that even those Protestants who most desire a racially united church—Negroes as well as whites—will not be willing to purchase their desire by methods which would immediately destroy a component part of the nature of

Protestant church government. Believing as they do that the will of God is best wrought within the tensions permitted by democracy, that the fruits of Christian fellowship grow best in a soil fertilized by voluntariness, that Christian community is an area of human relationship into which men must be wooed but cannot be compelled, Protestants must find some way other than force to heal the racial wound in the Body of Christ. Official Protestant bodies and their officers, conferences and conventions, and the ministers of local churches must address this issue in the spirit exhibited by Paul when he returned a presumably co-operative slave, Onesimus, to his owner, Philemon: ". . . but I preferred to do nothing without your consent in order that your goodness might not be by compulsion but of your own free will."[3] There is, as we have seen, a vast area of human intercourse in which men must fortify justice, but Christian fellowship is a realm beyond justice and beyond the coercive power of state or church.

The third extra-racial factor which in white Protestant churches permits and even fosters a division of the races combines two characteristics: the familial nature and social function of Protestant church life and the complete freedom of the individual white Protestant to attend the church of his choice. These characteristics, each good in itself, need not but often do form by their combination patterns of social stratification and exclusiveness. Let us look for a moment at each one and then suggest how in combination they fashion a resistance to racial integration in the church.

It should be noted first that the public worship of all Christians is to some extent horizontal as well as vertical; that is, it establishes a relationship not only between the communicant and his God but also between communicant and communicant. Diagrammatically it could be said that Christian public worship is always to some extent triangular; there are lines which flow from each communicant to the object of common worship. These lines converge in God and in the symbolic representation of God: altar or

[3] Philemon, verse 14.

communion table, priest or pastor, candle or Bible, crucifix or cross. But there is a base which completes this triangle: the sense of community which embraces those who are in common worship, the line of spiritual communication which relates to each other all those who share a mutual worship.

Protestants seem to have a monopoly on the word *fellowship,* but they do not have a monopoly on the experience. Even so, for the Protestant the horizontal line in the diagram of public worship is broad and heavy. He requires for his complete spiritual satisfaction worship in a church where he knows and is known by the membership of that church and usually considers himself a mere visitor rather than a full communicant when he worships in other churches. He needs not only a God to worship but also a sense of close relationship, filial relationship, between himself and those who with him worship God. This line of Christian community flows not only through Protestant worship but also through the total and extensive relationship of the Protestant to his church. For example, the dining or fellowship hall is assumed to be an essential part of the church edifice, and the activities centering in this hall are second in importance only to those which take place in the sanctuary.

For most Protestants the church, then, is his second and larger home. If we can think of the home as the social unit which forms the inmost circle surrounding the individual, we can then consider that for the Protestant the church is the next larger concentric social unit encircling his family and himself. What the Negro church is for Negro life, the white church to a far less but still significant degree is for the white Protestant: the principal social center of his life. This is not to imply that there is not among non-Protestants a sense of solidarity; but it is to say that among Protestants the sense of solidarity is in its scope and intensity a requisite of church life. To most Protestants the church is *koinonia* rather than *ekklesia.*

That there is merit and strength in this concept of the nature and role of the church, that it provides in the church social settings which test and nurture the Christian compassions and the Christian ethic, that at its best it approximates that oneness which Christ desired for his disciples—all this we take for granted. Nevertheless, in this strength there is a weakness. The familial nature and social function of the white Protestant churches, encouraging as they do an intense and intimate fellowship within the church, tempt the members of the local church to place a premium upon social similarity and acceptability. The horizontal relationships—those which relate people to people—begin to take priority over those which relate people to God. The church thus begins to fall short of genuine Christian community, substituting for it a fellowship of congeniality; and, whereas Christian community allows for no exclusions on the basis of taste, a fellowship of mere congeniality requires such exclusions. Thus the exclusiveness which may properly belong to the smaller family, the home, intrudes itself into the larger family, the church, where it does not properly belong; and the churches become stratified along social and economic lines and segregated along racial lines.

This stratification and segregation of the Protestant churches, moreover, is made possible and, indeed, is encouraged by the right of the individual Protestant to attend and to belong to the church of his choice. The Roman Catholic must support and is expected to attend the church serving the parish within which he lives, whether or not that church also serves an undesirable social element to which he refuses a personal relationship to himself and to his family. The Protestant, on the other hand, is bound by no parochial restrictions but may select, on whatever grounds appeal to him, the church which he and his family will call their own. The factors determining his choice are multiple, of course; but frequently the decision is based not upon distance or doctrine but upon the general social, cultural, and economic status of the preferred church. Thus a freedom which guarantees his right to profess his faith on the basis of conscience—his right to worship God according to the dictates of his own spiritual needs—is easily perverted into a license by which he escapes the claims of conscience—his refusal to accept into his Christian fellowship all whom God has accepted.

It must be noted also that it is natural for a people desiring racial distinctiveness to impose the exclusive patterns of their own personal lives upon as many of the surrounding social and civic relationships of life as possible. If the outer rings of defense against racial integration are numerous, the day when racial integration will make its demands upon the personal lives of the prejudiced is postponed. Therefore they extend the exclusive spirit and patterns of their own personal lives and their home life into their church life, the next larger and concentric social unit. By such Christians the segregated church is viewed as both a physical and a psychological sanitary cordon which, if kept racially pure, will surround and protect their family life and their individual lives from infiltration by socially and racially undesirable people. The next larger ring of defense against racial desegregation, the segregated public school, has been breached or is under serious threat; the segregated church remains for its racially sensitive members as the last bulwark against their own personal involvement in the integrating of the races. Their fear—erroneous but real—is that the collapse of segregation in the church will necessarily open their homes and their private lives to the claims of integration.

Moreover, so long as the church remains segregated, people have upon their own racial exclusiveness the silent, tacit blessing of that institution which is their moral guardian but which, by concurring in their racial behavior, justifies their personal exclusion of the Negro from areas of life where he rightfully belongs. Whatever the church may *say* in its lofty and idealistic pronouncements, the members of that church find their own racial exclusiveness buttressed and justified by what their local church *does*.

The nature and the function of white Protestant churches being what they are, it follows that the integration of the races within such churches not only will require the mutual occupation of a common space, the joining of voices in worship and prayer, the sharing of a hymnal, but will require that all areas of Christian community be opened to all members of the Christian family. Even now many white churches that will not exclude Negroes from their services of public worship either by force or by slurring suggestion will nevertheless stoutly resist the admission of Negroes into the membership of the church and into those social associations which membership in a Protestant church implies. In both a figurative and an actual sense it is true that the ultimate test of the sincerity and the thoroughness of racial integration in Protestant churches will be made not in the sanctuary where men share a mutual worship but in the fellowship hall where they break bread together.

The herculean task of the white Protestant churches as they face a racially divided Christendom is to preserve their stress upon the role of the church as a family of Christians who are in covenant with one another and with God and at the same time to welcome into all the social associations of such a fellowship all who profess Christ as Lord and Saviour, irrespective of their race or social status. As individual prejudices linger and the pressure for integration in the churches is intensified, the temptation will be for Protestant churches to forgo their familial quality and social function so that Negroes may be accepted into membership without offense to the prejudiced. If this tempting course is followed, the fellowship of the church will become broad only by becoming shallow. If, however, the Protestant churches meet and accept the challenge of racial integration without altering their concept of the nature and the role of the church, then the racial integration of Christians can find its fullest and most meaningful expression within the fellowship offered by Protestant churches.

We have noted three sets of factors which are themselves extraracial but which nevertheless hinder racial integration within Protestant churches: divisive factors common to white and Negro churches, divisive factors peculiar to Negro churches, and divisive factors peculiar to white churches. We see that the dilemma posed by the racially divided churches is therefore a tough and knotty problem which has been further complicated by nonracial and nontheological factors. The racially divided church is a historical and socio-psychological phenomenon which waits upon but will not be solved solely by the removal of racial prejudice within the church. The racially separate churches will therefore disappear only as the total social and religious climate that now naturally sustains them is replaced by a climate in which they can exist only as forced and artificial social structures. The required climatic changes can be put in the following order.

The first phase of the problem described those divisions which appear to be racial and which, indeed, had their origin in racial prejudice but are now actually ecclesiastical rather than racial in their nature. The cleavages, we have found, follow a racial line but upon analysis show themselves to be a part of the general denominational conflict within Protestantism. To this problem we do not need to bring any suggested remedies other than those which are being ably proposed by the many proponents of ecumenicity. Two observations, however, are pertinent. The ecumenical movement within Protestantism must not concentrate its attention and its unifying powers upon those churches which are divided by tradition, doctrine, and polity to such an extent that it ignores those churches which are divided solely by race. In addition, those Christians who are primarily concerned about racial unity must be governed in their policies and tempered in their expectations by the fact that some of the forces keeping Negro and white churches sundered from each other lie outside the realm of racial prejudice and racial hostility. In a word, the solution of racial division in the church depends to some extent upon the solution of the denominational fragmentation of Protestantism.

Secondly, the climatic change prerequisite to racial unity in the church must eliminate the necessity for the separate Negro church as a voice and instrument of racial justice. This can occur in one of three ways. Idealistically we can hope that the oppression of the Negro as a second-class citizen in American society will be so reduced by the various forces presently attacking such oppression that this role on the part of the Negro church will no longer be required. Again, and idealistically, we can hope that the conscience of white Christians will be so captured by the plight of the Negro as to make the white church willing to identify itself thoroughly with the economic, civic, and cultural struggles of the Negro. If the whole church were wholly concerned about the whole man and all men; if, as it should be, the church were truly the church of the people; if it were catholic in its embrace and compassion, there would obviously be no need for a special branch of the church dedicated to the particular needs of a particular people. Or, finally and more probably, as the Negro church is displaced in power and influence by those secular Negro and Negro-white organizations which are dedicated exclusively to the civic, social, and economic advancement of the Negro, the Negro church will become expendable as the voice and instrument of racial justice. Such a development, to be sure, is still somewhat remote; but the indications are that the N.A.A.C.P., the Urban League, the Negro press, and Negro clubs are steadily assuming that protesting role which formerly belonged almost exclusively to the Negro church. We must expect, however, as has now been repeatedly emphasized, that so long as the Negro church is required as a voice and instrument of racial justice, it will remain. Therefore the well-intentioned white Christian has a second duty and a second program. If he is sincerely committed to an elimination of racial division in the church, he must co-operate wholeheartedly with all social and civic agencies which seek to remove discrimination against the Negro.

In the third place, the climatic change prerequisite to a racially united church would mean that the Negro has been so thoroughly absorbed into the various forms of national life that the racial church serves no longer as the primary "social cosmos" of Negro life. If, and as, such times ripen, the Negro church can go the way of those bilingual churches and those hyphenated, Old Country-American clubs which were once so popular with immigrant

Americans but which now dwindle as social forms in American life. Certainly the time when the racial church will no longer be needed by the Negro as a social refuge is still distant; the areas of American life from which the Negro is still ostracized are many, and the social pressures which drive him back upon himself are obstinate. Here, then, the third duty and program of the white Christian is indicated if he is sincerely concerned about the racial rupture of the church. He must make it his purpose to break the color barrier in those social and civic organizations to which he belongs and from which the Negro is excluded solely on the grounds of race.

Thus we have pointed up the fact that an excluding white church, a discriminating white social order, and a segregating white society all combine to make essential to the Negro his racially separate church. Therefore the divisive factors peculiar to Negro churches can be removed only by decisive changes in the white man's church, the white man's state, and the white man's society. We have noted that there are in the existence and the multiple character of the Negro church conditions which make for division but which can be eliminated only by the will and the deed of the white man. Whatever else it is and may become, the Negro church is a protest and a rebuke, neither of which can end until the evils of discrimination and segregation are radically reduced. That reduction of racial oppression which will make feasible the gradual disappearance of the separate Negro church is a possibility over which the white man has principal control and for which he has primary responsibility.

These closing words have heavily stressed the fact that the racial cleavage existing between the churches has become in our day something more than a graphic expression of racial prejudice. They have warned those Christians who are embarrassed by and seek the removal of the racial line in the Christian church that their task is immensely complicated by factors beyond as well as within the areas of race and prejudice. They have urged upon such

Christians a realistic acceptance of the fact that the nonracial factors are stubborn and will preclude any early restoration of the racial oneness of the church. They have directed Christians to strive not only for an early erasure of racial prejudice in the Christian community but also for an alteration of those social patterns which are only indirectly related to the racial conflict within the church but nevertheless compound and perpetuate that conflict. They have shown that the scope and complexity of the problem require something more than pious pleas that Christians be Christian in their race relations.

Nevertheless, as we come to the final word, we must underscore once more the persistent and paramount fact that there is no hope whatsoever for a racially united church until the fundamental void between Negro and white Christians—their spiritual estrangement—is sincerely and broadly bridged and until genuine evidence of the restored oneness of all Christians becomes plain and actual in the full acceptance of Negro Christians into the whole Christian community. There is nothing to be gained—indeed, there is much to be lost—by placing Negroes in a white Christian church in which they will be subjected once again to those humiliations which originally gave the church its racial division. The Christian program seeking an end to racial division in the church must obviously move on a broad front and employ varied strategies; but none of these strategies, however necessary they may be, will succeed if they leave the invisible enemy unchallenged. Therefore the climatic change necessary for the racial integration of Christians within the church will mean that any Negro who chooses to do so can enter any Christian church as a worshiper or as an applicant for membership, not only with complete confidence that he will be warmly welcomed and accepted, but also with a full expectation that he will find in such a religious setting opportunities for the fullest expression and development of himself as a religious creature, opportunities unlimited by color or caste and restricted only by his own personal gifts and potentialities.

Index

219

Haselden, Kyle.

The racial problem in Christian perspective. ₁1st ed.₁
New York, Harper ₁1950₁

222 p.   22 cm.   (Rauschenbusch lectures)

Bibliographical footnotes.

1. Race problems.   ɪ. Title.   (Series: Rauschenbusch lectures,
Colgate-Rochester Divinity School, Rochester, N. Y.)

HT1521.H3   301.451   59–7150

Library of Congress